ZEN BUDDHISM & PSYCHOANALYSIS

ZEN BUDDHISM &

D. T. Suzuki, Erich Fromm,

PSYCHOANALYSIS

AND Richard De Martino

HARPER COLOPHON BOOKS

Harper & Row, Publishers

New York, Hagerstown, San Francisco, London

First HARPER COLOPHON edition published 1970 by Harper & Row, Publishers.

LIBRARY OF CONGRESS CATALOG CARD NUMBER: 60-5293

86 87 88 89 90   20 19 18 17 16

CONTENTS

FOREWORD

This book has its origin in a workshop on Zen Buddhism and Psychoanalysis, which was held under the auspices of the Department of Psychoanalysis of the Medical School, Autonomous National University of Mexico, during the first week of August, 1957, in Cuernavaca, Mexico.[1]

Any psychologist, even twenty years ago, would have been greatly surprised—or shocked—to find his colleagues interested in a "mystical" religious system such as Zen Buddhism. He would have been even more surprised to find that most of the people present were not just "interested" but deeply concerned, and that they discovered that the week spent with Dr. Suzuki and his ideas had a most stimulating and refreshing influence on them, to say the least.

[1] The conference was attended by about fifty psychiatrists and psychologists from both Mexico and the United States (the majority of them psychoanalysts). Aside from the papers published here, a number of other papers were given and discussed:

Dr. M. Green, "The Roots of Sullivan's Concept of Self."
Dr. J. Kirsch, "The Role of the Analyst in Jung's Psychotherapy."
Dr. I. Progoff, "The Psychological Dynamism of Zen."
        "The Concept of Neurosis and Cure in Jung."
Miss C. Selver, "Sensory Awareness and Body Functioning."
Dr. A. Stunkard, "Motivation for Treatment."
Dr. E. Tauber, "Sullivan's Concept of Cure."
Dr. P. Weisz, "The Contribution of Georg W. Groddeck."

We publish in this book only the ones which had the most direct connection with Zen Buddhism, partly for reasons of space, and partly because, without publishing the discussions which were held, the other papers would not be sufficiently unified.

The reason for this change lies in factors which are discussed later on in the book, especially in my paper. To sum them up briefly, they are to be found in the development of psychoanalytic theory, in the changes that have occurred in the intellectual and spiritual climate of the Western world, and in the work of Dr. Suzuki, who, by his books, his lectures, and his personality, has made the Western world acquainted with Zen Buddhism.

Every participant in the conference was expected to have some acquaintance with Dr. Suzuki's writings, just as many a reader of this volume may have. What distinguishes his lectures published here from his other writings, is the fact that they deal specifically with psychological problems such as the unconscious, and the self, and furthermore that they were addressed to a small group of psychoanalysts and psychologists whose questions and concerns were made known to Dr. Suzuki during the discussions and conversations of a whole week spent together. As a result these lectures will, I believe, be of particular value to psychiatrists and psychologists and to many other thoughtful people interested in the problem of man, because while they do not make "easy reading" they nevertheless guide the reader to an understanding of Zen Buddhism to a point where he should be able to continue on his own.

The two other parts of this book hardly need any comment. It should only be mentioned that while Dr. Suzuki's and Mr. De Martino's papers are almost completely literal versions of their lectures (in Dr. Suzuki's paper only the direct form of a "lecture address" has been changed into the one of a written paper), my own paper has been completely revised, both in length and in content. The main reason for this revision lies in the conference itself. While I was acquainted with the literature on Zen Buddhism, the stimulation of the conference and subsequent thinking led me to a considerable enlargement and revision of my ideas. This refers not only to my understanding of Zen, but also to certain psychoanalytic concepts, such as the problems of what constitutes the unconscious, of the transformation of the unconscious into consciousness, and of the goal of psychoanalytic therapy.

ERICH FROMM

ZEN BUDDHISM & PSYCHOANALYSIS

LECTURES ON ZEN BUDDHISM

by D. T. Suzuki

I. EAST AND WEST

Many able thinkers of the West, each from his specific point of view, have dealt with this timeworn topic, "East and West," but so far as I know there have been comparatively few Far Eastern writers who have expressed their views as Easterners. This fact has led me to choose this subject as a kind of preliminary to what will follow.

Basho (1644-94), a great Japanese poet of the seventeenth century, once composed a seventeen-syllable poem known as *haiku* or *hokku*. It runs, when translated into English, something like this:

> When I look carefully
> I see the *nazuna* blooming
> By the hedge!

> *Yoku mireba*
> *Nazuna hana saku*
> *Kakine kana.*

It is likely that Basho was walking along a country road when he noticed something rather neglected by the hedge. He then approached closer, took a good look at it, and found it was no less than a wild plant, rather insignificant and generally unnoticed by passers-by. This is a plain fact described in the

1

poem with no specifically poetic feeling expressed anywhere except perhaps in the last two syllables, which read in Japanese *kana*. This particle, frequently attached to a noun or an adjective or an adverb, signifies a certain feeling of admiration or praise or sorrow or joy, and can sometimes quite appropriately be rendered into English by an exclamation mark. In the present *haiku* the whole verse ends with this mark.

The feeling running through the seventeen, or rather fifteen, syllables with an exclamation mark at the end may not be communicable to those who are not acquainted with the Japanese language. I will try to explain it as best I can. The poet himself might not agree with my interpretation, but this does not matter very much if only we know that there is somebody at least who understands it in the way I do.

First of all, Basho was a nature poet, as most of the Oriental poets are. They love nature so much that they feel one with nature, they feel every pulse beating through the veins of nature. Most Westerners are apt to alienate themselves from nature. They think man and nature have nothing in common except in some desirable aspects, and that nature exists only to be utilized by man. But to Eastern people nature is very close. This feeling for nature was stirred when Basho discovered an inconspicuous, almost negligible plant blooming by the old dilapidated hedge along the remote country road, so innocently, so unpretentiously, not at all desiring to be noticed by anybody. Yet when one looks at it, how tender, how full of divine glory or splendor more glorious than Solomon's it is! Its very humbleness, its unostentatious beauty, evokes one's sincere admiration. The poet can read in every petal the deepest mystery of life or being. Basho might not have been conscious of it himself, but I am sure that in his heart at the time there were vibrations of feeling somewhat akin to what Christians may call divine love, which reaches the deepest depths of cosmic life.

The ranges of the Himalayas may stir in us the feeling of sublime awe; the waves of the Pacific may suggest something of infinity. But when one's mind is poetically or mystically or religiously opened, one feels as Basho did that even in every blade of wild grass there is something really transcending all venal, base human feelings, which lifts one to a realm equal in

its splendor to that of the Pure Land. Magnitude in such cases
has nothing to do with it. In this respect, the Japanese poet has
a specific gift that detects something great in small things,
transcending all quantitative measurements.

This is the East. Let me see now what the West has to offer
in a similar situation. I select Tennyson. He may not be a
typical Western poet to be singled out for comparison with the
Far Eastern poet. But his short poem here quoted has something very closely related to Basho's. The verse is as follows:

> Flower in the crannied wall,
> I pluck you out of the crannies;—
> Hold you here, root and all, in my hand,
> Little flower—but if I could understand
> What you are, root and all, and all in all,
> I should know what God and man is.

There are two points I like to notice in these lines:

1. Tennyson's plucking the flower and holding it in his
hand, "root and all," and looking at it, perhaps intently. It is
very likely he had a feeling somewhat akin to that of Basho who
discovered a *nazuna* flower by the roadside hedge. But the
difference between the two poets is: Basho does not pluck the
flower. He just looks at it. He is absorbed in thought. He
feels something in his mind, but he does not express it. He
lets an exclamation mark say everything he wishes to say. For
he has no words to utter; his feeling is too full, too deep, and he
has no desire to conceptualize it.

As to Tennyson, he is active and analytical. He first plucks
the flower from the place where it grows. He separates it from
the ground where it belongs. Quite differently from the
Oriental poet, he does not leave the flower alone. He must
tear it away from the crannied wall, "root and all," which
means that the plant must die. He does not, apparently, care
for its destiny; his curiosity must be satisfied. As some medical
scientists do, he would vivisect the flower. Basho does not even
touch the *nazuna,* he just looks at it, he "carefully" looks at
it—that is all he does. He is altogether inactive, a good contrast
to Tennyson's dynamism.

I would like to notice this point specifically here, and may have occasion to refer to it again. The East is silent, while the West is eloquent. But the silence of the East does not mean just to be dumb and remain wordless or speechless. Silence in many cases is as eloquent as being wordy. The West likes verbalism. Not only that, the West transforms the word into the flesh and makes this fleshiness come out sometimes too conspicuously, or rather too grossly and voluptuously, in its arts and religion.

2. What does Tennyson do next? Looking at the plucked flower, which is in all likelihood beginning to wither, he proposes the question within himself, "Do I understand you?" Basho is not inquisitive at all. He feels all the mystery as revealed in his humble *nazuna*—the mystery that goes deep into the source of all existence. He is intoxicated with this feeling and exclaims in an unutterable, inaudible cry.

Contrary to this, Tennyson goes on with his intellection: "*If* [which I italicize] I could understand you, I should know what God and man is." His appeal to the understanding is characteristically Western. Basho accepts, Tennyson resists. Tennyson's individuality stands away from the flower, from "God and man." He does not identify himself with either God or nature. He is always apart from them. His understanding is what people nowadays call "scientifically objective." Basho is thoroughly "subjective." (This is not a good word, for subject always is made to stand against object. My "subject" is what I like to call "absolute subjectivity.") Basho stands by this "absolute subjectivity" in which Basho sees the *nazuna* and the *nazuna* sees Basho. Here is no empathy, or sympathy, or identification for that matter.

Basho says: "look carefully" (in Japanese "*yoku mireba*"). The word "carefully" implies that Basho is no more an onlooker here but the flower has become conscious of itself and silently, eloquently expressive of itself. And this silent eloquence or eloquent silence on the part of the flower is humanly echoed in Basho's seventeen syllables. Whatever depth of feeling, whatever mystery of utterance, or even philosophy of "absolute subjectivity" there is, is intelligible only to those who have actually experienced all this.

In Tennyson, as far as I can see, there is in the first place no depth of feeling; he is all intellect, typical of Western mentality.

He is an advocate of the Logos doctrine. He must say something, he must abstract or intellectualize on his concrete experience. He must come out of the domain of feeling into that of intellect and must subject living and feeling to a series of analyses to give satisfaction to the Western spirit of inquisitiveness.

I have selected these two poets, Basho and Tennyson, as indicative of two basic characteristic approaches to reality. Basho is of the East and Tennyson of the West. As we compare them we find that each bespeaks his traditional background. According to this, the Western mind is: analytical, discriminative, differential, inductive, individualistic, intellectual, objective, scientific, generalizing, conceptual, schematic, impersonal, legalistic, organizing, power-wielding, self-assertive, disposed to impose its will upon others, etc. Against these Western traits those of the East can be characterized as follows: synthetic, totalizing, integrative, nondiscriminative, deductive, nonsystematic, dogmatic, intuitive, (rather, affective), nondiscursive, subjective, spiritually individualistic and socially group-minded,[1] etc.

When these characteristics of West and East are personally symbolized, I have to go to Lao-tse (fourth century B.C.), a great thinker in ancient China. I make him represent the East, and what he calls the multitudes may stand for the West. When I say "the multitudes" there is no intention on my part to assign the West in any derogatory sense to the role of Lao-tsean multitudes as described by the old philosopher.

Lao-tse portrays himself as resembling an idiot. He looks as if he does not know anything, is not affected by anything. He is practically of no use in this utilitarianistic world. He is almost expressionless. Yet there is something in him which makes him not quite like a specimen of an ignorant simpleton. He only outwardly resembles one.

The West, in contrast to this, has a pair of sharp, penetrating eyes, deep-set in the sockets, which survey the outside world

[1] Christians regard the church as the medium of salvation because it is the church that symbolizes Christ who is the savior. Christians are related to God not individually but through Christ, and Christ is the church and the church is the place where they gather to worship God and pray to him through Christ for salvation. In this respect Christians are group-minded while socially they espouse individualism.

as do those of an eagle soaring high in the sky. (In fact, the eagle is the national symbol of a certain Western power.) And then his high nose, his thin lips, and his general facial contour —all suggest a highly developed intellectuality and a readiness to act. This readiness is comparable to that of the lion. Indeed, the lion and the eagle are the symbols of the West.

Chuang-tze of the third century B.C. has the story of *konton (hun-tun)*, Chaos. His friends owed many of their achievements to Chaos and wished to repay him. They consulted together and came to a conclusion. They observed that Chaos had no sense organs by which to discriminate the outside world. One day they gave him the eyes, another day the nose, and in a week they accomplished the work of transforming him into a sensitive personality like themselves. While they were congratulating themselves on their success, Chaos died.

The East is Chaos and the West is the group of those grateful, well-meaning, but undiscriminating friends.

In many ways the East no doubt appears dumb and stupid, as Eastern people are not so discriminative and demonstrative and do not show so many visible, tangible marks of intelligence. They are chaotic and apparently indifferent. But they know that without this chaotic character of intelligence, their native intelligence itself may not be of much use in living together in the human way. The fragmentary individual members cannot work harmoniously and peacefully together unless they are referred to the infinite itself, which in all actuality underlies every one of the finite members. Intelligence belongs to the head and its work is more noticeable and would accomplish much, whereas Chaos remains silent and quiet behind all the superficial turbulence. Its real significance never comes out to become recognizable by the participants.

The scientifically minded West applies its intelligence to inventing all kinds of gadgets to elevate the standard of living and save itself from what it thinks to be unnecessary labor or drudgery. It thus tries hard to "develop" the natural resources it has access to. The East, on the other hand, does not mind engaging itself in menial and manual work of all kinds, it is apparently satisfied with the "undeveloped" state of civilization. It does not like to be machine-minded, to turn itself into a slave to the machine. This love of work is perhaps characteristic of the East. The story of a farmer as told by Chuang-tze is highly significant and suggestive in many senses, though the incident is supposed to have taken place more than two thousand years ago in China.

Chuang-tze was one of the greatest philosophers in ancient China. He ought to be studied more than he is at present. The Chinese people are not so speculative as the Indian, and are apt to neglect their own thinkers. While Chuang-tze is very well known as the greatest stylist among Chinese literary men, his thoughts are not appreciated as they deserve. He was a fine collector or recorder of stories that were perhaps prevalent in his day. It is, however, likely that he also invented many tales to illustrate his views of life. Here is a story, which splendidly illustrates Chuang-tze's philosophy of work, of a farmer who refused to use the shadoof to raise water from his well.

A farmer dug a well and was using the water for irrigating his farm. He used an ordinary bucket to draw water from the well, as most primitive people do. A passer-by, seeing this, asked the farmer why he did not use a shadoof for the purpose; it is a labor-saving device and can do more work than the primitive method. The farmer said, "I know it is labor-saving and it is for this very reason that I do not use the device. What I am afraid of is that the use of such a contrivance makes one machine-minded. Machine-mindedness leads one to the habit of indolence and laziness."

Western people often wonder why the Chinese people have not developed many more sciences and mechanical contrivances. This is strange, they say, when the Chinese are noted for their discoveries and inventions such as the magnet, gunpowder, the wheel, paper, and other things. The principal reason is that the Chinese and other Asiatic peoples love life as it is lived and do not wish to turn it into a means of accomplishing something else, which would divert the course of living to quite a different channel. They like work for its own sake, though, objectively speaking, work means to accomplish something. But while working they enjoy the work and are not in a hurry to finish it. Mechanical devices are far more efficient and accomplish more. But the machine is impersonal and non-creative and has no meaning.

Mechanization means intellection, and as the intellect is primarily utilitarian there is no spiritual estheticism or ethical spirituality in the machine. The reason that induced Chuang-tze's farmer not to be machine-minded lies here. The machine hurries one to finish the work and reach the objective for which it is made. The work or labor in itself has no value except as the means. That is to say, life here loses its creativity and turns into an instrument, man is now a goods-producing mechanism. Philosophers talk about the significance of the person; as we see now in our highly industrialized and mechanized age the machine is everything and man is almost entirely reduced to thralldom. This is, I think, what Chuang-tze was afraid of. Of course, we cannot turn the wheel of industrialism back to the primitive handicraft age. But it is well for us to be mindful of the significance of the hands and also of the evils attendant on the mechanization of modern life, which emphasizes the intellect too much at the expense of life as a whole.

So much for the East. Now a few words about the West. Denis de Rougemont in his *Man's Western Quest* mentions "the person and the machine" as characterizing the two prominent features of Western culture. This is significant, because the person and the machine are contradictory concepts and the West struggles hard to achieve their reconciliation. I do not know whether Westerners are doing it consciously or unconsciously. I will just refer to the way in which these two heterogeneous ideas are working on the Western mind at present. It is to be remarked that the machine contrasts with Chuang-tze's philosophy of work or labor, and the Western ideas of individual freedom and personal responsibility run counter to the Eastern ideas of absolute freedom. I will not go into details. I will only try to summarize the contradictions the West is now facing and suffering under:

1. The person and the machine involve a contradiction, and because of this contradiction the West is going through great psychological tension, which is manifested in various directions in its modern life.

2. The person implies individuality, personal responsibility, while the machine is the product of intellection, abstraction, generalization, totalization, group living.

3. Objectively or intellectually or speaking in the machine-

minded way, personal responsibility has no sense. Responsibility is logically related to freedom, and in logic there is no freedom, for everything is controlled by rigid rules of syllogism.

4. Furthermore, man as a biological product is governed by biological laws. Heredity is fact and no personality can change it. I am born not of my own free will. Parents give birth to me not of their free will. Planned birth has no sense as a matter of fact.

5. Freedom is another nonsensical idea. I am living socially, in a group, which limits me in all my movements, mental as well as physical. Even when I am alone I am not at all free. I have all kinds of impulses which are not always under my control. Some impulses carry me away in spite of myself. As long as we are living in this limited world, we can never talk about being free or doing as we desire. Even this desire is something which is not our own.

6. The person may talk about freedom, yet the machine limits him in every way, for the talk does not go any further than itself. The Western man is from the beginning constrained, restrained, inhibited. His spontaneity is not at all his, but that of the machine. The machine has no creativity; it operates only so far or so much as something that is put into it makes possible. It never acts as "the person."

7. The person is free only when he is not a person. He is free when he denies himself and is absorbed in the whole. To be more exact, he is free when he is himself and yet not himself. Unless one thoroughly understands this apparent contradiction, he is not qualified to talk about freedom or responsibility or spontaneity. For instance, the spontaneity Westerners, especially some analysts, speak about is no more and no less than childish or animal spontaneity, and not the spontaneity of the fully mature person.

8. The machine, behaviorism, the conditioned reflex, Communism, artificial insemination, automation generally, vivisection, the H-bomb—they are, each and all, most intimately related, and form close-welded solid links of a logical chain.

9. The West strives to square a circle. The East tries to equate a circle to the square. To Zen the circle is a circle, and the square is a square, and at the same time the square is a circle and the circle a square.

10. Freedom is a subjective term and cannot be interpreted objectively. When we try, we are surely involved inextricably in contradictions. Therefore, I say that to talk about freedom in this objective world of limitations all around us is nonsense.

11. In the West, "yes" is "yes" and "no" is "no"; "yes" can never be "no" or vice versa. The East makes "yes" slide over to "no" and "no" to "yes"; there is no hard and fast division between "yes" and "no." It is in the nature of life that it is so. It is only in logic that the division is ineradicable. Logic is human-made to assist in utilitarianistic activities.

12. When the West comes to realize this fact, it invents such concepts known in physics as complementarity or the principle of uncertainty when it cannot explain away certain physical phenomena. However well it may succeed in creating concept after concept, it cannot circumvent facts of existence.

13. Religion does not concern us here, but it may not be without interest to state the following: Christianity, which is the religion of the West, talks of Logos, Word, the flesh, and incarnation, and of tempestuous temporality. The religions of the East strive for excarnation, silence, absorption, eternal peace. To Zen incarnation is excarnation; silence roars like thunder; the Word is no-Word, the flesh is no-flesh; here-now equals emptiness *(śūnyatā)* and infinity.

II. THE UNCONSCIOUS IN ZEN BUDDHISM

What I mean by "the unconscious" and what psychoanalysts mean by it may be different, and I have to explain my position. First, how do I approach the question of the unconscious? If such a term could be used, I would say that my "unconscious" is "metascientific" or "antescientific." You are all scientists and I am a Zen-man and my approach is "antescientific"—or even "antiscientific" sometimes, I am afraid. "Antescientific" may not be an appropriate term, but it seems to express what I wish it to mean. "Metascientific" may not be bad, either, for the Zen position develops after science or intellectualization has occupied for some time the whole field of human study; and Zen demands that before we give ourselves up unconditionally to the scientific sway over the whole field of human activities we stop and reflect within ourselves and see if things are all right as they are.

The scientific method in the study of reality is to view an object from the so-called objective point of view. For instance, suppose a flower here on the table is the object of scientific study. Scientists will subject it to all kinds of analyses, botanical, chemical, physical, etc., and tell us all that they have found out about the flower from their respective angles of study, and say that the study of the flower is exhausted and that there is nothing more to state about it unless something new is discovered accidentally in the course of other studies.

The chief characteristic, therefore, which distinguishes the scientific approach to reality is to describe an object, to talk *about* it, to go *around* it, to catch anything that attracts our sense-intellect and abstract it *away* from the object itself, and when all is supposedly finished, to synthesize these analytically formulated abstractions and take the outcome for the object itself.

But the question still remains: "Has the complete object been really caught in the net?" I would say, "Decidedly not!" Because the object we think we have caught is nothing but the sum of abstractions and not the object itself. For practical and utilitarian purposes, all these so-called scientific formulas seem to be more than enough. But the object, so-called, is not all there. After the net is drawn up, we find that something has escaped its finer meshes.

There is, however, another way, which precedes the sciences or comes after them, to approach reality. I call it the Zen approach.

1.

The Zen approach is to enter right into the object itself and see it, as it were, from the inside. To know the flower is to become the flower, to be the flower, to bloom as the flower, and to enjoy the sunlight as well as the rainfall. When this is done, the flower speaks to me and I know all its secrets, all its joys, all its sufferings; that is, all its life vibrating within itself. Not only that: along with my "knowledge" of the flower I know all the secrets of the universe, which includes all the secrets of

my own Self, which has been eluding my pursuit all my life so
far, because I divided myself into a duality, the pursuer and
the pursued, the object and the shadow. No wonder that I
never succeeded in catching my Self, and how exhausting this
game was!

Now, however, by knowing the flower I know my Self. That
is, by losing myself in the flower I know my Self as well as the
flower.

I call this kind of approach to reality the Zen way, the ante-
scientific or metascientific or even antiscientific way.

This way of knowing or seeing reality may also be called
conative or creative. While the scientific way kills, murders
the object and by dissecting the corpse and putting the parts
together again tries to reproduce the original living body,
which is really a deed of impossibility, the Zen way takes life as
it is lived instead of chopping it to pieces and tying to restore
its life by intellection, or in abstraction gluing the broken
pieces together. The Zen way preserves life as life; no surgical
knife touches it. The Zen poet sings:

> All is left to her natural beauty,
> Her skin is intact,
> Her bones are as they are:
> There is no need for the paints, powders of any tint.
> She is as she is, no more, no less.
> How marvelous!

The sciences deal with abstractions and there is no activity
in them. Zen plunges itself into the source of creativity and
drinks from it all the life there is in it. This source is Zen's
Unconscious. The flower, however, is unconscious of itself. It
is I who awaken it from the unconscious. Tennyson misses it
when he plucks it from the crannied wall. Basho has it when
he looks at the shyly blooming *nazuna* by the wild hedge. I
cannot tell just where the unconscious is. Is it in me? Or is it
in the flower? Perhaps when I ask, "Where?" it is nowhere. If
so, let me be in it and say nothing.

While the scientist murders, the artist attempts to recreate.
The latter knows reality cannot be reached by dissection. He
therefore uses canvas and brush and paints and tries to create

out of his unconscious. When this unconscious sincerely and genuinely identifies itself with the Cosmic Unconscious, the artist's creations are genuine. He has really created something; his work is not a copy of anything; it exists in its own right. He paints a flower which, if it is blooming from his unconscious, is a new flower and not an imitation of nature.

The abbot of a certain Zen monastery wished to have the ceiling of the Dharma Hall decorated with a dragon. A noted painter was asked to do the work. He accepted, but complained that he had never seen a real dragon, if such really existed. The abbot said, "Don't mind your not having seen the creature. You become one, you be transformed into a living dragon, and paint it. Don't try to follow the conventional pattern."

The artist asked, "How can I become a dragon?" Replied the abbot, "You retire to your private room and concentrate your mind on it. The time will come when you feel that you must paint one. That is the moment when you have become the dragon, and the dragon urges you to give it a form."

The artist followed the abbot's advice, and after several months' strenuous strivings he became confident of himself because of his seeing himself in the dragon out of his unconscious. The result is the dragon we see now on the ceiling of the Dharma Hall at the Myoshinji, Kyoto.

Incidentally, I want to mention another story of a dragon's encounter with a Chinese painter. This painter wished to paint a dragon but, not having seen a live one yet, he longed for a good opportunity. One day a real one looked in from the window and said, "Here I am, paint me!" The painter was so overtaken by this unexpected visitor that he fainted, instead of looking carefully at it. No picture of a live dragon came out of him.

The seeing is not enough. The artist must get into the thing and feel it inwardly and live its life himself. Thoreau is said to have been a far better naturalist than professional ones. So was Goethe. They knew nature just because of their being able to live it. The scientists treat it objectively, that is, superficially. "I and thou" may be all right, but we cannot in truth say that; for as soon as we say it "I" am "thou" and "thou" art "I." Dualism can hold itself only when it is backed by something that is not dualistic.

Science thrives on dualism; therefore, scientists try to reduce everything into quantitative measurements. For this purpose they invent all kinds of mechanical appliances. Technology is the keynote of modern culture. Anything that cannot be reduced to quantification they reject as not scientific, or as ante-scientific. They set up a certain set of rules, and things that elude them are naturally set aside as not belonging to their field of study. However fine the meshes, as long as they are meshes some things are sure to escape them and these things, therefore, cannot be measured in any way. Quantities are destined to be infinite, and the sciences are one day to confess their inability to inveigle Reality. The unconscious is outside the field of scientific study. Therefore, all that the scientists can do is point to the existence of such a field. And that is enough for science to do.

The unconscious is something to feel, not in its ordinary sense, but in what I would call the most primary or fundamental sense. This may need an explanation. When we say, "I feel the hard table," or "I feel chilly," this sort of feeling belongs in the domain of the senses, distinguishable from such senses as hearing or seeing. When we say, "I feel lonely," or "I feel exalted," this is more general, more totalistic, more innerly, but it still belongs in the field of relative consciousness. But the feeling of the unconscious is much more basic, primary, and points to the age of "Innocence," when the awakening of consciousness out of the so-called chaotic Nature has not yet taken place. Nature, however, is not chaotic, because anything chaotic cannot exist all by itself. It is simply a concept given to the realm which refuses to be measured by the ordinary rules of ratiocination. Nature is chaotic in the sense that it is the reservoir of infinite possibilities. The consciousness evolved out of this chaos is something superficial, touching only the fringe of reality. Our consciousness is nothing but an insignificant floating piece of island in the Oceanus encircling the earth. But it is through this little fragment of land that we can look out to the immense expanse of the unconscious itself; the feeling of it is all that we can have, but this feeling is not a small thing, because it is by means of this feeling that we can realize that our fragmentary existence gains its full significance, and thus that we can rest assured that we are not living in vain.

Science, by definition, can never give us the sense of complete security and fearlessness which is the outgrowth of our feeling of the unconscious.

We cannot all be expected to be scientists, but we are so constituted by nature that we can all be artists—not, indeed, artists of special kinds, such as painters, sculptors, musicians, poets, etc., but artists of life. This profession, "artist of life," may sound new and quite odd, but in point of fact we are all born artists of life and, not knowing it, most of us fail to be so and the result is that we make a mess of our lives, asking, "What is the meaning of life?" "Are we not facing blank nothingness?" "After living seventy-eight, or even ninety years, where do we go? Nobody knows," etc., etc. I am told that most modern men and women are neurotic on this account. But the Zen-man can tell them that they all have forgotten that they are born artists, creative artists of life, and that as soon as they realize this fact and truth they will all be cured of neurosis or psychosis or whatever name they have for their trouble.

2.

What then is meant by being an artist of life?

Artists of any kind, as far as we know, have to use one instrument or another to express themselves, to demonstrate their creativity in one form or another. The sculptor has to have stone or wood or clay and the chisel or some other tools to impress his ideas on the material. But an artist of life has no need of going out of himself. All the material, all the implements, all the technical skill that are ordinarily required are with him from the time of his birth, perhaps even before his parents gave him birth. This is unusual, extraordinary, you may exclaim. But when you think about this for a while you will, I am sure, realize what I mean. If you do not, I will be more explicit and tell you this: the body, the physical body we all have, is the material, corresponding to the painter's canvas, the sculptor's wood or stone or clay, the musician's violin or flute, the singer's vocal cords. And everything that is attached to the body, such as the hands, the feet, the trunk of the body, the head, the viscera, the nerves, the cells, thoughts, feelings, senses—everything, indeed, that goes to make up the whole personality—is both the material on which and the instruments with which the person molds his creative genius into conduct, into behavior, into all forms of action, indeed into life itself. To such a person his life reflects every image he creates out of his inexhaustive source of the unconscious. To such, his every deed expresses originality, creativity, his living personality. There is in it no conventionality, no conformity, no inhibitory motivation. He moves just as he pleases. His behavior is like the wind which bloweth as it listeth. He has no self encased in his fragmentary, limited, restrained, egocentric existence. He is gone out of this prison. One of the great Zen masters of the T'ang says: "With a man who is master of himself wherever he may be found he behaves truly to himself." This man I call the true artist of life.

His Self has touched the unconscious, the source of infinite possibilities. His is "no-mind." Says St. Augustine, "Love God and do what you will." This corresponds to the poem of Bunan, the Zen master of the seventeenth century:

> While alive
> Be a dead man,
> Thoroughly dead;
> And act as you will,
> And all is good.

To love God is to have no self, to be of no-mind, to become "a dead man," to be free from the constrictive motivations of consciousness. This man's "Good morning" has no human element of any kind of vested interest. He is addressed and he responds. He feels hungry and eats. Superficially, he is a natural man, coming right out of nature with no complicated ideologies of modern civilized man. But how rich his inward life is! Because it is in direct communion with the great unconscious.

I do not know if it is correct to call this kind of unconscious the Cosmic Unconscious. The reason I like to call it so is that what we generally call the relative field of consciousness vanishes away somewhere into the unknown, and this unknown, once recognized, enters into ordinary consciousness and puts in good order all the complexities there which have been tormenting us to greater or lesser degrees. The unknown thus gets related to our mind, and, to that extent, unknown, and mind must be somehow of the same nature and cherish a mutual communication. We can thus state that our limited consciousness, inasmuch as we know its limitation, leads us to all sorts of worry, fear, unsteadiness. But as soon as it is realized that our consciousness comes out of something which, though not known in the way relative things are known, is intimately related to us, we are relieved of every form of tension and are thoroughly at rest and at peace with ourselves and with the world generally. May we not call this unknown the Cosmic Unconscious, or the source of infinite creativity whereby not only artists of every description nourish their inspirations, but even we ordinary beings are enabled, each according to his natural endowments, to turn his life into something of genuine art?

The following story may illustrate to a certain extent what I mean by transforming our everyday life into something of an art. Dogo of the eighth century was a great Zen master of the T'ang dynasty. He had a young disciple who wished to be taught Zen. He stayed with the master for some time but there was no specific teaching. One day he approached the master and said, "I have been with you for quite a while, but I have had no instruction. Why so? Please be good enough to advise me." The master said, "Why! I have been instructing you in Zen ever since you came to me." Protested the disciple, "Pray tell me what instruction it was." "When you see me in the morning you salute me, and I return it. When the morning meal is brought, I accept it gratefully. Where do I not point out the essence of the mind?" Hearing this, the disciple hung his head and seemed to be absorbed in deciphering the meaning of the master's words. The master then told him, "As soon as you begin thinking about it, it is no more there. You must see it im-mediately, with no reasoning, with no hesitation." This is said to have awakened the disciple to the truth of Zen.

The truth of Zen, just a little bit of it, is what turns one's humdrum life, a life of monotonous, uninspiring commonplaceness, into one of art, full of genuine inner creativity.

There is in all this something which antedates the scientific study of reality, something which cannot be scooped up in the meshes of the scientifically constructed apparatus.

The unconscious in its Zen sense is, no doubt, the mysterious, the unknown, and for that reason unscientific or ante-scientific. But this does not mean that it is beyond the reach of our consciousness and something we have nothing to do with. In fact it is, on the contrary, the most intimate thing to us, and it is just because of this intimacy that it is difficult to take hold of, in the same way as the eye cannot see itself. To become, therefore, conscious of the unconscious requires a special training on the part of consciousness.

Etiologically speaking, consciousness was awakened from the unconscious sometime in the course of evolution. Nature works its way unconscious of itself, and the conscious man comes out of it. Consciousness is a leap, but the leap cannot mean a dis-connection in its physical sense. For consciousness is in con-stant, uninterrupted communion with the unconscious. Indeed, without the latter the former could not function; it would lose its basis of operation. This is the reason why Zen declares that the Tao is "one's everyday mind." By Tao, Zen of course means the unconscious, which works all the time in our consciousness. The following *mondō* (question and answer) may help us to understand something of the Zen unconscious: When a monk asked a master what was meant by "one's every-day mind," he answered, "When hungry, I eat; when tired, I sleep."

I am sure you would ask: "If this is the unconscious you Zen-men talk about as something highly mysterious and of the greatest value in human life as the transforming agent, we cannot help doubting it. All those 'unconscious' deeds have long been relegated to our instinctive reflexive domain of con-sciousness in accordance with the principle of mental economy. We should like to see the unconscious connected with a much higher function of the mind, especially when, as in the case of a swordsman, this is attained only after long years of strenuous training. As to these reflexive acts, such as eating, drinking, sleeping, etc., they are shared by the lower animals as well as by infants. Zen certainly cannot value them as something the fully matured man has to strive to find meaning in."

Let us see whether or not there is any essential difference between the "instinctive" unconscious and the highly "trained" unconscious.

Bankei, one of the great modern Japanese Zen masters, used

to teach the doctrine of the Unborn. To demonstrate his idea he pointed to facts of our daily experience such as hearing a bird chirp, seeing a flower in bloom, etc., and said that these are all due to the presence in us of the Unborn. Whatever *satori*[2] there is, it must be based on this experience and no others, he concluded.

This seems to point superficially to the identification of our sense-domain and the highly metaphysical Unborn. In one sense the identification is not wrong, but in another sense it is. For Bankei's Unborn is the root of all things and includes not only the sense-domain of our daily experience but the totality of all realities past, present, and future and filling the cosmos to the ends of the ten quarters. Our "everyday mind," or our daily experience, or our instinctive acts, as far as they are considered in themselves, have no special value and significance. They acquire these only when they are referred to the Unborn or what I have called the "Cosmic Unconscious." For the Unborn is the fountainhead of all creative possibilities. It then so happens that when we eat it is not we who eat but the Unborn; when we sleep, tired, it is not we who sleep but the Unborn.

As long as the unconscious is an instinctive one, it does not go beyond that of animals or of infants. It cannot be that of the mature man. What belongs to the latter is the trained unconscious in which all the conscious experiences he has gone through since infancy are incorporated as constituting his whole being. For this reason, in the case of the swordsman, as soon as he takes up the sword his technical proficiency, together with his consciousness of the entire situation, recede into the background and his trained unconscious begins to play its part to the fullest extent. The sword is wielded as if it had a soul in itself.

Perhaps we can say this: the unconscious as far as it is related to the sense-domain is the outcome of a long process of evolution in the cosmical history of life, and it is shared alike by animals and infants. But as intellectual development takes place, as we grow up, the sense-domain is invaded by intellect and the naïveté of sense-experience is lost. When we smile, it is not just smiling: something more is added. We do not eat

[2] See below, p. 46, and also *Essays in Zen Buddhism*, first series, p. 227 *et seq.*

as we did in our infancy; eating is mixed with intellection. And as we all realize this invasion by the intellect or the mixing with intellect, simple biological deeds are contaminated by egocentric interest. This means that there is now an intruder into the unconscious, which can no longer directly or immediately move into the field of consciousness, and all deeds that have been relegated to biologically instinctive functions now assume the role of consciously and intellectually directed acts.

This transformation is known as the loss of "innocence" or the acquirement of "knowledge" in the usage of the Biblical myth. In Zen and Buddhism generally it is called "the affective contamination *(klesha)*" or "the interference of the conscious mind predominated by intellection *(vijñāna)*."

The mature man is now asked by Zen to cleanse himself of this affective contamination and also to free himself of the intellectual conscious interference if he sincerely wishes to realize a life of freedom and spontaneity where such disturbing feelings as fear, anxiety, or insecurity have no room to assail him. When this liberation takes place, we have the "trained" unconscious operating in the field of consciousness. And we know what Bankei's "Unborn" or the Chinese Zen master's "everyday mind" is.

3.

We are now ready to hear Takuan's advice to his swordsman disciple Yagyu Tajima-no-kami.

Takuan's advice is chiefly concerned with keeping the mind always in the state of "flowing," for he says when it stops anywhere that means the flow is interrupted and it is this interruption that is injurious to the well-being of the mind. In the case of a swordsman, it means death. The affective taint darkens the mirror of man's primary *prajñā,* and the intellectual deliberation obstructs its native activity. *Prajñā,* which Takuan calls "immovable *prajñā,*" is the directing agency of all our movements, inner as well as outer, and when it is obstructed the conscious mind is clogged and the sword, disregarding the native, free, spontaneous directive activity of the "immovable *prajñā,*" which corresponds to our unconscious, begins to obey the consciously acquired technical skill of the art. *Prajñā* is the immovable mover which unconsciously operates in the field of consciousness.

When the swordsman stands against his opponent, he is not to think of the opponent, nor of himself, nor of his enemy's sword-movements. He just stands there with his sword which, forgetful of all technique, is really only to follow the dictates of the unconscious. The man has effaced himself as the wielder of the sword. When he strikes, it is not the man but the sword in the hands of the unconscious that strikes. There are stories in which the man himself has not been aware of the fact that he has struck down the opponent—all unconsciously. The working of the unconscious is in many cases simply miraculous.

Let me give one instance: the Magnificent Seven.

There is a Japanese film play, recently introduced to American audiences, in which a scene is presented where the unemployed samurais are given a trial of their swordsmanship. This is fictitious, but there is no doubt that it is all based on facts of history. The leader of the whole enterprise contrived a certain way whereby each swordplayer was to be tested. He placed a village young man behind the entrance which must be passed by every comer to the building. As soon as a samurai tried to step over the threshold, the young man was to strike him suddenly with a stick and see how the newcomer behaved.

The first one was caught and received the stick coming down over him with its full force. He failed to pass the test. The second one dodged the blow and in return struck the young man. He was not thought good enough to pass. The third one stopped at the entrance and told the one behind the door not to try such a mean trick on a fully seasoned warrior. For this one sensed the presence of a secret enemy inside even before he actually detected him who was securely hidden. This was due to the long experience this samurai had had to go through in those turbulent days. He thus proved to be a successful candidate for the work that was to be carried out in the village.

This sensing of an unseen enemy seems to have developed among the swordsmen to a most remarkable degree of efficiency in those feudal days when the samurai had to be on the alert in every possible situation that might arise in his daily life. Even while in sleep he was ready to meet an untoward event.

I do not know if this sense could be called a sixth sense or a sort of telepathy and therefore a subject for parapsychology, so-called. One thing at least I wish to mention is that philosophers of swordplay ascribe this sense acquired by the swordsman to the working of the unconscious which is awakened when he attains a state of selflessness, of no-mind. They would say that when the man is trained to the highest degree of the art he has no more of the ordinary relative consciousness in which he realizes that he is engaged in the struggle for life and death, and that when this training takes effect his mind is like a mirror on which every thought that would be moving in the opponent's mind is reflected and he knows at once where and how to strike the opponent. (To be exact, this is not knowledge but an intuition taking place in the unconscious.) His sword moves, mechanically as it were, all by itself, over an opponent who finds defense impossible because the sword falls on the spot where the opponent is not at all on guard. The swordsman's unconscious is thus said to be the outcome of selflessness which, being in accord with the "Reason of Heaven and Earth," strikes down everything that is against this Reason. The race or the battle of swordsmanship is not to the swiftest or to the strongest or to the most skillful, but to the one whose mind is pure and selfless.

Whether or not we accept this interpretation is another question; the fact is that the master swordsman possesses what we may designate the unconscious and that this state of mind is attained when he is no more conscious of his acts and leaves everything to something which is not of his relative consciousness. We call this something or somebody; because of its being outside the ordinary field of consciousness we have no word for it except to give it a negative name, X, or the unconscious. The unknown, or X, is too vague, and as it comes in connection with consciousness in such a way that X avails itself of all the technical skill acquired consciously, it may be not inappropriately designated as the unconscious.

4.

What is the nature of this unconscious? Is it still in the field of psychology, though in its widest sense of the term? Is it somehow related to the source of all things, such as the

"Reason of Heaven and Earth," or something else which comes up in the ontology of Eastern thinkers? Or shall we call it "the great perfect mirror knowledge *(adarśanajñāna),*" as it is sometimes called by Zen masters?

The following incident told of Yagyu Tajima-no-kami Munenori, a disciple of Takuan, the Zen master, may not be directly related to the unconscious described in the preceding part of this lecture. One reason is that he is not actually facing the enemy. But it may not be a matter of indifference to the psychologist to find that a faculty which may almost be called parapsychic can be developed by going through a certain form of discipline. I may perhaps add that the case of Yagyu Tajima-no-kami has, of course, not been tested in a scientific way. But there are a number of such cases recorded in the annals of Japanese swordsmanship, and even in our modern experiences there is reason to believe in the probability of such "telepathic" intuition, while I must repeat that this kind of psychological phenomenon has probably nothing to do with the unconscious of which I have been talking.

Yagyu Takima-no-kami was one spring day in his garden admiring the cherry trees in full bloom. He was, to all appearances, deeply absorbed in contemplation. He suddenly felt a *sakki* [3] threatening him from behind. Yagyu turned around, but did not see any human being approaching except the young boy attendant who generally follows his lord carrying his sword. Yagyu could not determine the source from which emanated the *sakki*. This fact puzzled him exceedingly. For he had acquired after long training in swordplay a kind of sixth sense whereby he could detect at once the presence of *sakki*.

He soon retired into his room and tried to solve the problem, which annoyed him very much. For he had never made a

[3] *Sakki* literally means "air of murder." The swordsman frequently refers to this kind of incident. It is something indescribable, only felt inwardly as emanating from a person or an object. People often speak of the fact that some swords are filled with this "air of murder," whereas others inspire one with a sense of awe, or of reverence, or even of benevolence. This is generally ascribed to the character or temperament of the artist who wrought the sword, for works of art reflect the spirit of the artists, and in Japan the sword is not just a murderous weapon but a work of art. The *sakki* also comes out of a person who harbors covertly or manifestly the idea of killing somebody. This "air" is also said to hover over a detachment of soldiers intent on attacking the enemy.

mistake before in detecting and locating definitely the origin of *sakki* whenever he sensed its presence. He looked so annoyed with himself that all his attendants were afraid of approaching him to ask what was the matter.

Finally, one of the older servants came up to him to inquire if he were not feeling ill and in need of their help in one way or another. Said the lord, "No, I am not ill. But I have experienced something strange while out in the garden, which goes beyond my understanding. I am contemplating the matter." So saying, he told him the whole incident.

When the matter became known among the attendants, the young one who was following the lord came forward tremblingly and made this confession: "When I saw your lordship so absorbed in admiring the cherry blossoms, the thought came upon me: However skillful our lord may be in his use of the sword, he could not in all probability defend himself if I at this moment suddenly struck him from behind. It is likely that this secret thought of mine was felt by the lord." So confessing, the young one was ready to be punished by the lord for his unseemly thought.

This cleared up the whole mystery that had been troubling Yagyu so very much and the lord was not in the mood to do anything to the innocent young offender. He was satisfied by seeing that his feeling did not err.

III. THE CONCEPT OF THE SELF IN ZEN BUDDHISM

The Zen approach to reality which may be defined as antescientific is sometimes antiscientific in the sense that Zen moves entirely against the direction pursued by science. This is not necessarily saying that Zen is opposed to science, but simply that to understand Zen one has to take a position which has been hitherto neglected or rather ignored by scientists as "unscientific."

The sciences are uniformly centrifugal, extroverted, and they look "objectively" toward the thing they pick up for study. The position they thus assume is to keep the thing away from them and never to strive to identify themselves with the object of their study. Even when they look within for self-inspection they are careful to project outwardly what is within, thus making themselves foreign to themselves as if what is within did not belong to them. They are utterly afraid of being "subjective." But we must remember that as long as we stand outside we are outsiders, that for that very reason we can never know the thing itself, that all we can know is *about*—which means that we can never know what our real self is. Scientists, therefore, can never expect to reach the Self, however much they desire to. They can no doubt talk a great deal *about* it, and that is all they can do. Zen thus advises us to reverse the direction science is pursuing if we are really to get acquainted with the Self. It is said that the proper study of mankind is man, and in this case man is to be taken in the sense of Self, because it is mankind and not animalkind that can ever be conscious of Self. Men or women who do not aspire to the knowledge of the Self are, I am afraid, to go through another cycle of birth and death. "To know thyself" is to know thy Self.

Scientific knowledge of the Self is not real knowledge as long as it objectifies the Self. The scientific direction of study is to be reversed, and the Self is to be taken hold of from within and not from the outside. This means that the Self is to know itself without going out of itself. Some may ask, "How can that be possible? Knowledge always implies a dichotomy, the knower and the object known." I answer: "Self-knowledge is possible only when the identification of subject and object takes place; that is, when scientific studies come to an end, and lay down all their gadgets of experimentation, and confess that they cannot continue their researches any further unless they can transcend themselves by performing a miraculous leap over into a realm of absolute subjectivity."

The realm of absolute subjectivity is where the Self abides. "To abide" is not quite correct here, because it only suggests the statical aspect of the Self. But the Self is ever moving or becoming. It is a zero which is a staticity, and at the same time an infinity, indicating that it is all the time moving. The Self is dynamic.

The Self is comparable to a circle which has no circumference, it is thus *śūnyatā*, emptiness. But it is also the center of such a circle, which is found everywhere and anywhere in the circle. The Self is the point of absolute subjectivity which may convey the sense of immobility or tranquillity. But as this point can be moved anywhere we like, to infinitely varied spots, it is really no point. The point is the circle and the circle is the point. This apparently impossible miracle takes place when the direction science pursues is reversed and turns to Zen. Zen is indeed the performer of this impossibility.

Thus, as the Self moves from zero to infinity and from infinity to zero, it is in no way an object of scientific studies. As it is absolute subjectivity, it eludes all our efforts to locate it at any objectively definable spot. As it is so elusive and cannot be taken hold of, we cannot experiment with it in any scientific way. We cannot entrap it by any objectively constructed media. With all scientific talents this can never be performed, because it is not in the nature of things within their sphere of operation. The Self when properly adjusted knows how to discover itself without going through the process of objectification.

I referred before to de Rougemont's recent book, *Man's Western Quest,* in which he names "the person" and "the machine" as two of the features distinguishing the nature of the Western quest after reality. According to him, "the person" was first a legal term in Rome. When Christianity took up the question of the Trinity its scholars began to use it theologically, as is seen in such terms as "the divine person" and "the human person," which were harmoniously reconciled in Christ. As we use the term now, it has a moral-psychological connotation with all its historical implications. The problem of the person is finally reducible to that of the Self.

De Rougemont's person is dualistic in its nature, and some kind of conflict is always going on within itself. This conflict or tension or contradiction is what constitutes the essence of the person, and naturally it follows that the feeling of fear and uncertainty secretly accompanies every mode of activity it manifests. In fact, we can say that it is this very feeling that drives the person to commit unbalanced acts of passion and violence. Feeling is at the source of all human deeds, and not dialectical difficulties. Psychology comes first, then logic and analysis, and not vice versa.

According to de Rougemont, therefore, it is impossible for Western people to transcend the dualism residing in the very nature of the person as long as they cling to their historico-theological tradition of God-man or man-God. It is due to this

dualistic conflict in the unconscious and its resulting sense of
uneasiness that they venture out into time as well as into space.
They are thorough extroverts and not introverts. Instead of
looking into the nature of the person inwardly and taking hold
of it, they strive objectively to reconcile the dualistic conflicts
which they discern on the plane of intellection. As to the person itself, let me quote from de Rougemont. According to him:

The person is call and answer, it is action and neither fact nor
object, and the complete analysis of facts and objects will never
yield an indisputable proof of it. (p. 50)

The person is never here or there, but in an action, in a tension,
in an impetuous rush—more seldom as the source of a happy
balance, such as a work of Bach's gives the feeling of. (p. 55)

This sounds fine. The person is really what de Rougemont
describes and is in correspondence with what Buddhists would
say about the *ātman*, "is gone to dissolution *(visankara)*." But
what the Mahayanists feel like asking the author of the quo-
tations above cited is: "Who are *you* to say all these fine things
from the conceptual point of view? We like to interview *you*
personally, concretely, or existentially. When *you* say, 'So long
as I live, I live in contradiction,' who is this 'I'? When you tell
us that the fundamental antinomy of the person is to be taken
over by faith, who is the *one* who takes to this faith? Who is
the *one* who experiences this faith? Behind faith, experience,
conflict, and conceptualization there must be a live *man* who
does all this."

Here is the story of a Zen monk who directly and concretely
put his finger right on the person and let his inquirer see what
it was like. The monk came to be known later by the name
of Ōbaku Ki-un (died 850), one of the great Zen masters of the
T'ang dynasty. The governor of the district once visited a
monastery under his jurisdiction. The abbot took him to in-
spect the different parts of the premises. When they came to
a room where the portraits of the succeeding abbots were on
display, the governor pointed at one of them and asked the
abbot, "Who is this?" The abbot answered, "The late abbot."
The governor's second question was, "Here is his portrait, and
where is the person?" This was more than the abbot could

answer. The governor, however, insisted on having his question answered. The abbot was desperate, for he was unable to find anyone among his followers who could satisfy the governor. He finally happened to remember a strange monk who had recently come to the monastery for lodging and who spent most of his spare moments in keeping the courtyards well swept and in good order. He thought this stranger, who looked like a Zen monk, might be able to answer the governor. The monk was called in and introduced to the governor. The latter respectfully addressed the monk,

"Venerable Sir, these gentlemen around here are unfortunately not willing to answer my question. Will you be good enough to undertake the answering?"
The monk said, "What is your question?"
The governor told him all about what had happened before and repeated the question, "Here is the portrait of the former abbot, and where is the person?"
The monk at once called out, "O Governor!"
The governor responded, "Yes, Venerable Sir!"
"Where is he?" This was the monk's solution.

Scientists, including theologians and philosophers, like to be objective and avoid being subjective, whatever this may mean. For they firmly adhere to the view that a statement is true only when it is objectively evaluated or validated and not merely subjectively or personally experienced. They forget the fact that a person invariably *lives* a personal life and not a conceptually or scientifically defined one. However exactly or objectively or philosophically the definition might have been given, it is not the definition the person lives but the life itself, and it is this life which is the subject of human study. Objectivity or subjectivity is not the question here. What concerns us most vitally is to discover by ourselves, personally, where this life is, how it is lived. The person that knows itself is never addicted to theorization, never writes books, never indulges itself in giving instructions to others; it always lives its unique life, its free creative life. What is it? Where is it? The Self knows itself from within and never from the outside.
As we see in this story of Obaku and the governor, we are

ordinarily satisfied with the portrait or likeness, and, imagining the *man* dead, fail to ask the question asked by the governor, "Here is the portrait, and where is the person?" To translate the whole trend of the story into our modern way of saying things; "Existence (including the person) is sustained by the continual invention of relative solutions and of useful compromises." The idea of birth and death is a relative solution and portrait-making is a kind of sentimentally useful compromise. But as to the presence of an actual living personality, there is nothing of the sort, hence the governor's demand, "Where is the person?" Ōbaku was a Zen monk and lost no time in waking him from a dreamlike world of concepts with the call, "O Governor!" The answer came at once, "Yes, Venerable Sir!" We see here the whole person leaping out of the chamber of analysis, abstraction, and conceptualization. When this is understood we know who the person is, where he is, and who the Self is. If the person is identified with a mere action and no more, it is not a living one, it is an intellectualized one, it is not *my* Self, nor is it your Self.

Jōshū Jūshin (778-897) was once asked by a monk, "What is my Self?" Jōshū said, "Have you finished the morning gruel?" "Yes, I have finished." Jōshū then told him, "If so, wash your bowl." The eating is an act, the washing is an act, but what is wanted in Zen is the actor himself, is the eater and the washer that does the acts of eating and washing; and unless this person is existentially or experientially taken hold of, one cannot speak of the acting. Who is the one who is conscious of acting? and who is the one who communicates this fact of consciousness to you? and who are you who tell all this not only to yourself but to all others? "I," "you," "she," or "it" —all this is a pronoun standing for a somewhat behind it. Who is this somewhat?

Another monk asked Jōshū, "What is my Self?" Jōshū said, "Do you see the cypress tree in the courtyard?" It is not the seeing but the seer that Jōshū the master wants to have. If the Self is the axis of the spiral coils and is never objectified or factualized, it is still there, and Zen tells us to seize it with our naked hands and show to the master that which is unseizable, unobjectivizable, or unattainable (J. *fukatoku*, Ch. *pu-ko-te*, Skr. *anupalabdha*). Here lies, we can see, the discrepancy between science and Zen. Zen, however, we must remember, has no objection whatever to the scientific approach to reality; Zen only desires to tell scientists that theirs is not the only approach but that there is another approach which Zen claims to be more direct, more inward, and more real and personal, which they may call subjective but which is not so in the way they would designate or define.

Person, individual, Self, and ego—I use them in this lecture as synonymous. The person is moral or conative, the individual contrasts with a group of any sort, the ego is psychological, and the Self is both moral and psychological and also has a religious connotation.

From the Zen point of view, what uniquely, psychologically, distinguishes the experience of the self is that it is saturated with the feeling of autonomy, freedom, self-determination, and lastly creativity. Hōkōji asked Basō Dō-ichi (died 788), "Who is the person who stands all alone without a companion among the ten thousand things (dharma)?" Answered Baso, "I'll tell you when you swallow up the West River at one gulp." This is the kind of achievement the Self or the person performs. Those psychologists or theologians who talk about the bundle of successive perceptions or impressions, or about the Idea, or about the principle of unity, or the dynamic totality of subjective experience, or about the nonexistential axis of the curvilinear human activities are those who are running in the direction opposite to that of Zen. The harder they run the farther they go away from Zen. Therefore, I say that science or logic is objective and centrifugal while Zen is subjective and centripetal.

Somebody has remarked, "Everything without tells the individual that he is nothing, while everything within persuades him that he is everything." This is a remarkable saying, for it is the feeling every one of us has when he sits quietly and deeply looks into the inmost chamber of his being. Something is moving there and would whisper to him in a still small voice that he is not born in vain. I read somewhere again: "You are tried alone; alone you pass into the desert; alone you are sifted by the world." But let a man once look within in all sincerity, and he will then realize that he is not lonely, forlorn, and deserted; there is within him a certain feeling of a royally magnificent aloneness, standing all by himself and yet not separated from the rest of existence. This unique situation, apparently or objectively contradicting, is brought about when he approaches reality in the Zen way. What makes him feel that way comes from his personally experiencing creativity or originality which is his when he transcends the realm of intellection and abstraction. Creativity differs from mere dynamism. It is the hallmark of the self-determining agent called the Self.

Individuality is also important in marking off the Self, but it is more political and ethical and closely allied with the idea of responsibility. It belongs in the realm of relativities. It is liable to become associated with self-asserting power. It is always conscious of others and to that extent controlled by them. Where individualism is emphasized, the mutually restricting feeling of tension prevails. There is no freedom here, no spontaneity, but a deep, heavy atmosphere or inhibition, suppression, and oppression overpowers one and the result is psychological disturbance in all its varieties.

Individuation is an objective term distinguishing one from another. When the distinction becomes exclusive, the desire for power lifts its head and frequently becomes uncontrollable. When it is not too strong or when it is more or less negative, one becomes extremely conscious of the presence of comments or criticisms. This consciousness sometimes pushes us into the maw of miserable thralldom, reminding us of Carlyle's *Sartor Resartus*. "The philosophy of clothes" is a philosophy of the apparent world where everybody dresses for everybody else to make himself or herself appear other than himself or herself. This is interesting. But when it goes too far, one loses one's originality, makes oneself ridiculous, and turns into a monkey.

When this aspect of the Self grows up to become too prominent and overbearing, the real Self is pushed back and is frequently reduced to a non-entity, which means it is suppressed. And we all know what this suppression means. For the creative unconscious can never be suppressed; it will assert itself in one way or another. When it cannot assert itself in the way natural to it, it will break all the barriers, in some cases violently and in other cases pathologically. In either way the real Self is hopelessly ruined.

Worrying over this fact, Buddha declared the doctrine of

annatta or *nirātma* or non-ego to wake us from the dream of appearances. Zen Buddhism, however, was not quite satisfied with Buddha's somewhat negativistic way of presenting the doctrine, and proceeded to demonstrate it in the most affirmative and the most direct possible way so that Buddhist followers would make no mistake in their approach to reality. Let us give an example from Rinzai Gigen (died 867):

One day he gave this sermon: "There is the true man of no rank in the mass of naked flesh, who goes in and out from your facial gates [i.e., sense organs]. Those who have not yet testified [to the fact], look, look!"

A monk came forward and asked, "Who is this true man of no rank?"

Rinzai came down from his chair and, taking hold of the monk by the throat, said, "Speak, speak!"

The monk hesitated.

Rinzai let go his hold and said, "What a worthless dirt-stick this is!" [4]

"The true man of no rank" is Rinzai's term for the Self. His teaching is almost exclusively around this Man *(nin, jên)* or Person, who is sometimes called "the Way-man" *(dōnin* or *tao-jên)*. He can be said to be the first Zen master in the history of Zen thought in China who emphatically asserts the presence of this Man in every phase of our human life-activity. He is never tired of having his followers come to the realization of the Man or the real Self. The real Self is a kind of metaphysical self in opposition to the psychological or ethical self which belongs in a finite world of relativity. Rinzai's Man is defined as "of no rank" or "independent of" *(mu-ye, wu-i),* or "with no clothes on," [5] all of which makes us think of the "metaphysical" Self.

With this preliminary remark let us proceed to quote Rinzai rather extensively as regards his view of the Man or Person or Self, as I think here he expresses himself quite eloquently and

[4] Literally, "a dried-up stick of dirt." J. *kanshiketsu,* Ch. *kan-shih-chueh.* Kan=dry, *shi*=ordure, *ketsu*=stick.

[5] *Muye* (J.) and *wu-i* (Ch.) mean "independent" as well as "no clothes on." *Ye (i)* is in the first case "dependent" and in the second "clothes."

in a thoroughgoing way on the subject and will help us in
understanding the Zen concept of the Self.

*Rinzai on the Self, or "The One who is, at this moment,
right in front of us, solitarily, illuminatingly, in full awareness, listening to this talk on the Dharma."* [6]

1.

[After talking about the triple body of Buddha *(trikaya)*, Rinzai
went on:] All these, I am quite sure, are but shadows. O Venerable
Sirs! You must recognize the Man *(jên)* who plays with these
shadows, that he is the source of all Buddhas and the refuge the
followers of the Way take to wherever they may be.

It is neither your physical body nor your stomach or liver or
kidney, nor is it the emptiness of space, who is expounding the
Dharma and listening to it. Who is he then who understands all
this? This is the One who is right in front of you, in all awareness,
with no divisible shape, and in solitary brightness. This One
understands how to talk about the Dharma and how to listen to it.

When you can see this, you are not in any way different from
Buddha and the patriarchs. [One who thus understands] is not
interrupted throughout all periods of time. He is everywhere our
eyes can survey. Only because of our affective hindrances, the intuition is intercepted; because of our imaginations, Reality is subject
to differentiation. Therefore, suffering a variety of pains, we trans-
migrate in the triple world. According to my view, nothing is
deeper than [this One,] and it is by this that every one of us can
have his emancipation.

O Followers of the Way! The mind is formless and penetrates the
ten quarters. With the eyes it is the seeing; with the ears it is the
hearing; with the nose it senses odors; with the mouth it argues;
with the hands it seizes; with the legs it walks about.

2.

O Followers of the Way, the One who, at this moment, right in
front of us, brightly, in solitude, and in full awareness, is listening

[6] The following translations are from Rinzai's *Sayings*, known as *Rinzi
Roku.*

[to the talk on the Dharma]—this Man *(jên)* tarries nowhere wherever he may be, he passes through the ten quarters, he is master of himself in the triple world. Entering into all situations, discriminating everything, he is not to be turned away [from what he is].

He would in one thought-instant penetrate through the Dharma-world. When he meets Buddha he talks in the fashion of a Buddha; when he meets a patriarch he talks in the fashion of a patriarch; when he meets an arhat he talks in the fashion of an arhat; when he meets a hungry ghost he talks in the fashion of a hungry ghost.

Turning everywhere, he would peregrinate through every land and be engaged in teaching all beings and yet not be outside of one thought-instant.

Everywhere he goes, he remains pure, undefined, his light penetrates the ten quarters, and the ten thousand things are of one Suchness.

3.

What is the true understanding?

It is you who enter into all [situations]: the ordinary and the holy, the defiled and the pure; it is you who enter into all the Buddha-lands, into Maitreya's Tower, into the Dharma-world of Vairochana; and wherever you enter you manifest a land subject to [the four stages of becoming]: coming into existence, continuing to exist, destruction, and extinction.

Buddha, appearing in the world, revolved the great wheel of the Dharma and passed into nirvāna [instead of staying for ever in the world as we ordinary beings might have expected]. Yet there are no signs of his going-and-coming. If we try to trace his birth-and-death, nowhere do we find it.

Entering into the Dharma-world of the Unborn, he peregrinates through every land. Entering into the world of the Lotus-womb, he sees that all things are of Emptiness and have no reality. The only being that is is the Tao-man *(tao-jên)* who, depending on nothing, is this moment listening to [my] talk on the Dharma. And this Man is the mother of all Buddhas.

Thus, Buddha is born of that which is dependent on nothing. When that which is dependent on nothing is understood, Buddha, too, is found unobtainable.

When one gains this insight he is said to have the true understanding.

Learners, not knowing this, are attached to names and phrases and thus stand blocked by such names as the ordinary or the wise. When their view of the Way is thus obstructed, they cannot clearly see [the Way].

Even the twelve divisions of the Buddha's teaching are no more than words and expressions [and not realities]. Learners, not understanding this, are bent on extracting sense out of mere words and phrases. As they are all depending on something, they find themselves entangled in causation and cannot escape a cycle of births and deaths in the triple world.

If you wish to transcend birth-and-death, going-and-coming, and to be freely unattached, you should recognize the Man who is at this moment listening to this talk on the Dharma. He is the one who has neither shape nor form, neither root nor trunk, and who, having no abiding place, is full of activities.

He responds to all kinds of situations and manifests his activities, and yet comes out of nowhere. Therefore, as soon as you try to search for him he is far away; the nearer you approach the farther he turns away from you. "Secret" is his name.

4.

Only, there is the One who is right in front of all these followers of the Way, at this very moment, listening to my talk on the Dharma—it is he who is not burnt by fire, is not drowned in water, it is he who saunters about as if in a garden, even when entering in the three evil paths or into Naraka, it is he who would never suffer any karmic consequences even when entering into the realm of the hungry ghosts or of the animals. Why so? Because he knows no conditions to avoid.

If you love the wise and hate the ordinary, you will be sinking in the ocean of birth-and-death. The evil passions are because of the mind; when you have no mind, what evil passions will bind you? When you are not troubled with discriminations and attachments, you will in no time and without effort attain the Way. As long as you run about among your neighbors in a confused state of mind, you are bound to return to the realm of birth-and-death, by however many "innumerable kalpas" you may try to master the Way. It is better to be back in your monastery and peacefully to sit cross-legged in the meditation hall.

5.

O Followers of the Way! You who are at this present moment
listening to my talk on the Dharma are not the four elements
[which make up your body]. You are that which makes use of the
four elements. When you are able to see this [truth], you can then
be free in your coming-and-going. As far as I can see there is
nothing I would reject.

6.

[The master once gave the following sermon:]
What is requisite of learners of the Way is to have faith in themselves. Do not seek outwardly. When you do you are simply carried
away by unessential externalities and will find yourselves altogether
unable to discriminate right from wrong. There are Buddhas,
there are patriarchs, they may say, but these are no more than
mere verbal tracks left behind the real Dharma. If a man happens
to appear before you displaying a word or a phrase in its dualistic
complications, you are puzzled and start to cherish a doubt. Not
knowing what to do, you run to neighbors and friends making
inquiries in every direction. You are completely at a loss. Men
of great character are not to waste time thus engaging themselves
in arguments and idle talks regarding host and intruder, right and
wrong, matter and wealth.

As I [7] stand here, I am no respecter of monks and laymen. Who-
ever presents himself before me, I know where the visitor comes
from. Whatever he may try to assume, I know that he is invariably
based on words, attitudes, letters, phrases, all of which are no more
than a dream or a vision. I see only the Man who comes out
riding on all the situations that may arise; he is the mysterious
theme of all Buddhas.

The Buddha-situation cannot proclaim itself as such. It is this
Man of the Way (tao-jên or dōin) of nondependence who comes out
riding on the situation.

If a man comes to me and says, "I am seeking the Buddha,"
I come out in conformity with the situation of purity. If a man
comes to me and asks about the bodhisattva, I come out in accord-

---

[7] "I" throughout this sermon stands for the "Man" (jên) or "absolute subjectivity," to use my terminology.

ance with the situation of compassion *(maitrī or karunā)*. If a man
comes to me and asks about bodhi [or enlightenment], I come
out in accordance with the situation of incomparable beauty. If
a man comes to me and asks about nirvāna, I come out in accordance with the situation of serene quietude. The situations may vary
infinitely, but the Man varies not. So, [it is said], "[It] [8] takes
forms in accordance with conditions, like the moon reflecting itself
[variously] in water."

[A few words of explanation may be needed. God, as long as he
remains in himself, with himself, and for himself, is absolute subjectivity, *śūnyatā* itself. As soon as he begins to move, however, he
is creator, and the world with its infinitely varying situations or
conditions evolves. The original God or the Godhead has not been
left behind in his solitariness, he is in the manyness of things. It
is human reasoning which is time that so often causes us to forget
him and place him outside our world of time and space and causality. Buddhist terminology superficially differs widely from that
of Christianity, but when we go down deeply enough we find the
two currents cross one another or flow out of the same source.]

7.

O Followers of the Way, it is urgently needed that you should
seek the true understanding so that you can walk uninhibitedly
all over the world without being deluded by all those unhuman
spirits [that is, false leaders of Zen].

The aristocrat is he who is not burdened with anything, remaining in a state of nondoing. Nothing extraordinary marks his everyday life.

As soon as you turn outwardly to seek your own limbs among
your neighbors [as if you did not have them already with you],
you commit a fault. You may try to find the Buddha, but he is no
more than a name. Do you know the One who thus goes around
seeking [something somewhere]?

The Buddhas and patriarchs have appeared in the ten quarters
in the past, future, and present, and their object is no less than
seeking the Dharma. All the followers of the Way [bodhi] who are
at present employed in the study of the Way—they, too, are seeking

[8] "It" is inserted here because the Chinese original, as usual, omits the
subject. "It" stands for Reality or the Man or the Person or the Self.

the Dharma and nothing else. When they have it their task is finished. When they have it not, they will as ever go on transmigrating through the five paths of existence.

What is the Dharma? It is no other than the Mind. The Mind has no form and penetrates through the ten quarters and its activities are manifested right before us. People do not believe it. They try to discover its names and phrases, imagining that the Buddha-dharma is in them. How wide of the mark they are! It is like the distance between heaven and earth.

O Followers of the Way! What do you think my sermons are concerned with? They are concerned with the Mind which enters into ordinary people as well as into wise men, into defiled ones as well as into the pure, into worldly ones as well as into the unworldly.

The point is that you [9] are neither ordinary nor wise, neither worldly nor unworldly. And it is *you* who affixes names to the unworldly as well as to the worldly, to the ordinary as well as to the wise. Neither the worldly nor the unworldly, neither the wise nor the ordinary can affix a name to this Man *(jên)*.

O Followers of the Way! It is up to you to take hold of [this truth] and make free use of it. Do not get attached to names. [The truth] is called the mysterious theme.

8.

A man of great character is not expected to be led astray at all by other people. He is master of himself wherever he goes. As he stands all is right with him.

As soon as one thought of doubt enters, evil spirits come to occupy the mind. As soon as the bodhisattva cherishes a doubt, a good opportunity is given to the devil of birth-and-death. Only keep the mind from being stirred up, have no longing for the outside.

When conditions arise let them be illuminated. You just believe in the One who is acting at this very moment. He is not employing himself in any particularly specified fashion.

As soon as one thought is born in your mind, the triple world rises with all its conditions which are classifiable under the six

---

9 "You" here as elsewhere is used in the sense of "the Mind" manifesting itself in "the Man." "You" and "the Man" are here interchangeable.

sense-fields. As you go on acting as you do in response to the conditions, what is wanting in you?

In one thought-moment you enter into the defiled as well as into the pure, into Maitreya's Tower, into the Land of Three Eyes. Wherever you may thus walk, you see nothing but empty names.

9.

O Followers of the Way, difficult indeed it is to be really true to oneself! The Buddha-dharma is deep, obscure, and unfathomable, but when it is understood, how easy it is! I spend all day telling people what the Dharma is, but learners seem not at all concerned to pay any attention to my talk. How many thousand times they tread it under their feet! And yet it is an utter darkness to them.

[The Dharma] has no form whatever, and yet how clearly it is manifesting itself in its solitariness! As they are deficient, however, in faith, they strive to understand it by means of names and words. Half a century of their life is simply wasted by carrying a lifeless corpse from one door to another. They run wildly up and down through the whole country shouldering all the while a bag [filled with empty words of the half-witted masters]. Yamarāja, Lord of the Underworld, will surely some day ask them for all the sandals they have worn out.

O Venerable Sirs, when I tell you that there is no Dharma as long as you seek it outwardly, learners fail to understand me. They would now turn inwardly and search for its meaning. They sit cross-legged against the wall with the tongue glued to the upper palate and in a state of immovability. They think this is the Buddhist tradition practiced by the patriarchs. A great error is here committed. If you take a state of immovable purity for what is required of you, this is to recognize [the darkness of] Ignorance [10] for your lordship.[11] Says an ancient master, "The darkest abyss of tranquillity—this is indeed what one has to shudder at." This is no other than what has been said above. If [on the other hand] you

[10] *Avidyā* in Sanskrit.

[11] Immovability, purity, serenity, or tranquillity—they all refer to a state of consciousness where all thought waves of every kind uniformly subside. This is also called the dark abyss of Ignorance or of the Unconscious, and the Zen-man is told to avoid it by all means and not to imagine it to be the ultimate object of Zen discipline.

take motility for the right thing, all the plant world knows what
motility is. But this could not be called the Tao. Motility is the
nature of the wind, while immobility is the nature of the earth.
They both have no self-nature.

If you try to catch [the Self] while it moves, it will stand in a
state of immobility; if you try to catch it while it remains immobile,
it will go on moving. It is like the fish swimmng freely over the
surging waves in the deep. O Venerable Sirs, moving and not-
moving are two aspects of [the Self] when it is objectively viewed,
while it is no other than the Way-man *(tao-jên)* himself who is not
dependent on anything, it is he who freely makes use of [the two
aspects of reality], sometimes moving, sometimes not moving. . . .
[Most learners are caught in this dichotomous dragnet.] But if
there be a man who is, holding a view that goes beyond ordinary
thought patterns,[12] and he should come to *me, I* would act with
mv whole being.[18]

O Venerable Sirs, here lies, indeed, the point where learners
have to apply themselves wholeheartedly, for there is no room here
even for a breath of air to pass through. It is like a flash of light-
ning or like a spark of flint-stone striking the steel. [One winks
and] the whole thing passes away. If learners' eyes are vacantly
fixed, all is lost. As soon as the mind is applied to it, it slips away
from you; as soon as a thought is stirred it turns its back on you.
The understanding one will realize that it is right in front of him.[14]

O Venerable Sirs, carrying the bowl-bag and the body filled with
ordure,[15] you are running from door to door with the expectation

12 Generally, three classes of people—upper, middling, and lower—are mentioned in regard to their natural endowments or inherent capacities to understand Buddhist truths.

13 The Chinese original for "I" and its modifications is *shan-sêng (san-zó* in
Japanese), meaning "a mountain monk," by which Rinzai refers to himself. This
humble title is to be understood not just as referring to Rinzai as an individual
belonging to this world relatively limited in every way, but to Rinzai as an
enlightened man who lives in the transcendental realm of absolute subjectivity
or emptiness. A man or person in this realm does not move or behave himself
as a partitively individualized being, as a psychologically defined self, or as an
abstract idea, but moves with his whole being or personality. This will become
clearer as we go on.

14 "It" is supplied by the translator, and refers to the Dharma or Reality or
the Person or the Man or the Tao (the Way).

15 The bowl-bag is the bag containing a begging-bowl which is carried by
the traveling monk. The ordure-filled body is a contemptuous title given to a
monk whose eye has not yet opened to the Dharma and whose mind is filled
with empty names and idle thoughts. The latter are compared to the excreta

of finding somewhere Buddha and Dharma. But the One who thus at this moment goes around seeking something—do you know who this very one is? He is the most dynamic one except that he has no roots, no stems whatever. You may try to catch him, but he refuses to be gathered up; you may try to brush him away, but he will not be dispersed. The harder you strive after him the further he is away from you. When you no more strive after him, lo, he is right in front of you. His supersensuous voice fills your ear. Those who have no faith are wasting their precious life to no purpose.

O Followers of the Way, it is [he] who enters in one thought-instant into the world of the Lotus-womb, into the Land of Vairochana, into the Land of Emancipation, into the Land of Supernatural Powers, into the Land of Purity, into the Dharma-world. It is he who enters into the defiled as well as into the pure, into the ordinary as well as into the wise. It is also he who enters into the realm of animals and of hungry ghosts. Wherever he may enter, we cannot discover any trace of his birth-and-death, however much we may try to locate him. What we have is no more than those empty names; they are like hallucinatory flowers in the air. They are not worth our striving to take hold of. Gain and loss, yea and nay—all the dichotomies are at once to be dropped. . . .

As to the way I, the mountain monk, handle myself, whether in affirmation or in negation, it is in conformity with the true [understanding]. Sportively and supersensuously I enter freely into all situations and apply myself as if I were not at all engaged in anything. Whatever transformations may take place in my environment, they are unable to affect me. If anything should come to me with the idea of getting something from me, I just come out and see him. He fails to recognize me. I then put on several kinds of clothes, and the learners start to give their interpretations, unmindfully captivated by my words and phrases. They altogether lack the power of discrimination! They take to the clothes I wear and distinguish their various colorings: blue, yellow, red, or white. When I take them off and enter into a state of pure blankness, they are taken aback and are at a loss, and wildly running about they would say, I have no clothes on. I would then turn to them and say,

---

which ought not to be harbored inside the body. A monk ever intent on accumulating ideas not at all cogent to the realization is also called "the rice bag" or "the ill-smelling skin-bag."

"Do you recognize the Man who goes about wearing all kinds of clothes?" They now at last all of a sudden turn their heads around and recognize me [in form]!

O Venerable Sirs, beware of taking clothes [for realities]. Clothes are not self-determining; it is the Man that puts on various clothes: clothes of purity, clothes of no-birth, clothes of enlightenment [bodhi], clothes of nirvāna, clothes of patriarchs, clothes of Buddahood. O Venerable Sirs, what we have here are merely sounds, words, and they are no better than the clothes we change. The movements start from the abdominal parts and the breath passing through the teeth produces various sounds. When articulated they linguistically make sense. Thus we clearly realize that they are unsubstantial.

O Venerable Sirs, outwardly by means of sounds and words and inwardly by the changing of modes of consciousness we think, we feel, and these are all the clothes we dress ourselves with. Do not commit the mistake of taking the clothes people wear for realities. When you go on like this, even after the elapsing of an innumerable number of kalpas, you will remain experts on clothes and no more. You will have to wander around in the triple world and be revolving the wheel of births and deaths. Nothing is like living a life of nondoing, and an old master states:

> I meet [him] and yet know [him] not,
> I converse [with him] and yet am ignorant of [his] name.

The reason why these days learners are unable [to get to reality] is that their understanding does not go beyond names and words. What they do is write down in their precious notebooks words of some half-witted senile masters, and, after wrapping them up in a threefold way, no, in a fivefold way, put them securely in a bag. This is to keep other people away from their curious inspection. Thinking that these words of the masters embody the deep-theme [of the Dharma], they treasure them thus in a most respectful manner. What a grave blunder they are committing! Oh, the old dim-sighted followers! What kind of juice do they expect to come out of the old dried-up bones? There are some who do not know what's good and what's bad. Going through the various scriptures and after much speculation and calculation, they gather up some phrases [which they use for their own purposes]. It is like a man who, after having swallowed a lump of filth himself, vomits it and then passes it over to others. Those who, like a tattler, transmit a rumor from mouth to mouth will have to pass their whole life for nothing.

Sometimes they say, "We are humble monks," and when they are asked by others as to the what of Buddhist teaching, they just shut up and have nothing to say. Their eyes are as if looking into the darkness and their closed mouth resembles a bent shoulder pole.[16] Even when Maitreya's appearance in this world takes place, such ones are destined for another world; they will have to go to hell to suffer a painful life.

O Venerable Sirs, what do you seek by going around so busily from one place to another? The result will be just to make your soles flatter than ever. There are no Buddhas who can be taken hold of [by your wrongly directed efforts]. There is no Tao [i.e., bodhi] which can be attained [by your vain striving]. There is no Dharma which can be realized [by your idle fumbling]. As long as you search outwardly for a Buddha with form [such as the thirty-two marks of great manhood], you can never realize that he has no resemblance to you [that is, to your real Self]. If you wish to know what your original mind is, I will tell you that it is neither integrative nor disintegrative. O Venerable Sirs, the true Buddha has no shape, the true Tao [or bodhi] has no substance, the true Dharma has no form. These three are merged in the oneness [of Reality]. Those minds that are still unable to understand this are subject to the unknown destiny of karma-consciousness.

IV. THE KOAN

1.

A koan is a kind of problem which is given by the master to his disciples to solve. "Problem" is not a good term, however, and I prefer the original Japanese Kō-an (kung-an in Chinese). Kō literally means "public" and an is "a document." But "a public document" has nothing to do with Zen. The Zen

---

[16] This is a wooden or sometimes a bamboo pole about six feet long used for carrying things over the shoulder. When the load is too heavy the pole bends. Rinzai sarcastically likens the monk's closed mouth to the pole thus bent.

"document" is the one each one of us brings along to this world at his birth and tries to decipher before he passes away.

According to Mahayana legend Buddha is said to have made the following utterance when he came out of his mother's body: "Heaven above, earth below, I alone am the most honored one." This was Buddha's "document" bequeathed to us to read, and those who read it successfully are the followers of Zen. There is, however, no secrecy in this, as it is all open or "public" to us, to every one of us; and to those who have an eye to see the utterance it presents no difficulty. If there is any hidden meaning in it at all, it is on our side and not in "the document."

The koan is within ourselves, and what the Zen master does is no more than to point it out for us so that we can see it more plainly than before. When the koan is brought out of the unconscious to the field of consciousness, it is said to have been understood by us. To effect this awakening, the koan sometimes takes a dialectical form but frequently assumes, superficially at least, an entirely nonsensical form.

The following may be classified as dialectical:
The master generally carries a staff or stick which is used while traveling over the mountain paths. But nowadays it has turned into a symbol of authority in the hand of the master, who frequently resorts to it to demonstrate his point. He will produce it before the congregation and say something like this: "This is not a staff. What do you call it?" Sometimes he may make this kind of statement: "If you say it is a staff, you 'touch' [or affirm]; if you do not call it a staff, you 'go against' [or negate]. Apart from negation and affirmation, what would you call it?" In fact, such a koan as this is more than dialectical. Here is one of the solutions given by a competent disciple: Once, when the master gave this statement, a monk came out of the congregation and, taking the staff away from the master, broke it into two and threw the pieces down on the ground.

There was another master who, bringing out his staff, made this enigmatic declaration: "When you have a staff, I'll give you one; when you have none I'll take it away from you."

Sometimes the master will ask quite legitimately, "Where do you come from?" or "Whither do you go?" But he may suddenly change his topic and say, "How my hands resemble those of the Buddha! And how my legs resemble those of the donkey!"

One may ask, "What does it matter if my hands are like those of the Buddha? As to my legs looking like those of the donkey, the statement sounds fantastic. Granting that they do, what has this fact to do with the ultimate question of existence, with which we are seriously concerned?" The questions or challenges here set down by the master may be regarded as "nonsensical" if you want to so designate them.

Let me give one or two more examples of such "nonsense" given by another master. When a disciple asked, "Who is the one who stands all alone, without a companion among the ten thousand things?" The master answered, "When you swallow the West River at one gulp, I'll tell you." "Impossible" will be our immediate reaction. But history tells us that this remark from the master opened up the dark chamber of the questioner's consciousness.

It was the same master who kicked the chest of a questioning monk whose fault was to ask, "What is the meaning of Bodhidharma's coming to China from the West?" which is tantamount to "What is the ultimate meaning of the Dharma?" But when the monk rose from the ground, recovering from the shock, he, boldly but most heartily laughing, declared, "How strange that every possible form of *samādhi* there is in the world is at the tip of a hair and I have mastered its secret meaning down to its deepest root!" What possible relationship could ever exist between the master's kick and the monk's daring pronouncement? This can never be understood on the plane of intellection. Nonsensical though all this may be, it is only from our habit of conceptualization that we miss facing the ultimate reality as it stands nakedly by itself. What is "nonsensical" indeed has a great deal of meaning and makes us penetrate the veil that exists as far as we stay on this side of relativity.

2.

These "questions and answers" (known as *mondō* in Japanese) and the masters' declarations which are now designated as koans were not known as such in the days when they actually took place; they were just the way that seekers of the truth used to become illumined and that masters of Zen resorted to for the sake of the questioning monks. What we may call a somewhat systematic way of studying Zen started with the masters of the Sung some time in the twelfth century. One of them selected what is known as Jōshū's *"Mu!"* (*wu* in Chinese) as a koan and gave it to his disciples to meditate upon it. The story of Jōshū's *"Mu!"* runs as follows:

Jōshū Jūshin (778-897, Chao-chou Ts'ung-shên in Chinese) was one of the great Zen masters of the T'ang dynasty. He was once asked by a monk, "Has a dog the Buddha-nature?" Answered the master, *"Mu!"* *"Mu!"* (*wu*) literally means "no." But when it is used as a kōan the meaning does not matter, it is simply *"Mu!"* The disciple is told to concentrate his mind on the meaningless sound *"Mu!"* regardless of whether it means "yes" or "no" or, in fact, anything else. Just *"Mu!"* *"Mu!"* *"Mu!"*

This monotonous repetition of the sound *"Mu!"* will go on until the mind is thoroughly saturated with it and no room is left for any other thought. The one who thus utters the sound, audibly or inaudibly, is now completely identified with the sound. It is no more an individual person who repeats the *"Mu!"*; it is the *"Mu!"* itself repeating itself. When he moves it is not he as a person conscious of himself but the *"Mu!"* The *"Mu!"* stands or sits or walks, eats or drinks, speaks or remains silent. The individual vanishes from the field of consciousness, which is now thoroughly occupied with the *"Mu!"* Indeed, the whole universe is nothing but the *"Mu!"* "Heaven above, earth below, I alone am the most honored one!" The *"Mu!"* is this "I." We now can say that the *"Mu!"* and the "I" and the Cosmic Unconscious—the three are one and the one is three. When this state of uniformity or identity prevails, the consciousness is in a unique situation, which I call "consciously unconscious" or "unconsciously conscious."

But this is not yet a *satori* experience. We may regard it as corresponding to what is known as *samādhi,* meaning "equilibrium," "uniformity," or "equanimity," or "a state of tranquillity." For Zen this is not enough; there must be a certain awakening which breaks up the equilibrium and brings one back to the relative level of consciousness, when a *satori* takes

place. But this so-called relative level is not really relative; it
is the borderland between the conscious level and the unconscious. Once this level is touched, one's ordinary consciousness
becomes infused with the tidings of the unconscious. This is
the moment when the finite mind realizes that it is rooted in
the infinite. In terms of Christianity, this is the time when the
soul hears directly or inwardly the voice of the living God.
The Jewish people may say that Moses was in this state of mind
at Mount Sinai when he heard God announcing his name as
"I am that I am."

3.

The question now is, "How did the Sung masters discover
the 'Mu!' to be an effective means leading to the Zen experience?" There is nothing intellectual in the "Mu!" The situation is quite contrary to that which took place when the
mondō were exchanged between masters and disciples before
the Sung era. Indeed, wherever there is any question, the
very fact of questioning implies intellectualization. "What is
Buddha?" "What is the Self?" "What is the ultimate principle
of the Buddhist teaching?" "What is the meaning of life?" "Is
life worth living?" All these questions seem to demand a certain "intellectual" or intelligible answer. When these questioners are told to go back to their rooms and apply themselves
to the "study" of the "Mu!" how would they take it? They
would simply be dumfounded and not know what to make of
the proposition.

While all this is true, we must remember that the position of
Zen is to ignore all kinds of questioning because the questioning itself is against the spirit of Zen and that what Zen expects
of us is to lay hands on the questioner himself as a person and
not anything that comes out of him. One or two examples will
amply prove the point.

Basō Dō-ichi was one of the greatest masters of Zen in the
T'ang dynasty; in fact, we can say that Zen really made a start
with him. His treatment of questioners was something most
revolutionary and most original. One of them was Suiryo (or
Suiro), who was kicked down by the master when Suiryo asked

him about the truth of Zen.[17] On another occasion Baso struck
a monk who happened to wish to know the first principle of
Buddhism. On a third occasion he gave a slap over the ear to
one whose fault was asking the master, "What is the meaning
of Bodhidharma's visit to China?" [18] Superficially, all these
rough handlings on the part of Baso have nothing to do with
the questions asked, unless they are to be understood as a kind
of punishment inflicted on those who were silly enough to
propose such vitally interesting questions. And the strange
thing is that the monks concerned were not at all offended or
irate. On the contrary, one of them was so overwhelmed with
joy and excitement that he declared, "How most strange that
all the truths given out in the Sūtras are manifested at the tip
of a hair!" How could a master's kick on the monk's chest
effect such a miracle of transcendental nature?

Rinzai, another great Zen master, was noted for his giving
the unintelligible utterance "Kātz!" when a question was asked.
Toku-san, still another great one, used to wield his staff freely
even before a monk opened his mouth. In fact, Toku-san's
famous declaration runs thus: "Thirty blows of my stick when
you have something to say; thirty blows just the same when you
have nothing to say." As long as we remain on the level of
relativity or intelligibility, we cannot make anything out of
those actions on the part of the master; we cannot discover
any sort of relationship between the questions that may be
asked by the monks and what seems to be an impetuous outburst of an irascible personality, to say nothing of the effect this
outburst has upon the questioners. The incoherency and in-
comprehensibility of the whole transaction is, to say the least,
bewildering.

4.

The truth is that what involves the totality of human existence is not a matter of intellection but of the will in its most
primary sense of the word. The intellect may raise all kinds of
questions—and it is perfectly right for it to do so—but to expect
any final answer from the intellect is asking too much of it,
for this is not in the nature of intellection. The answer lies

[17] See above and also my *Living by Zen* (London, Rider, 1950) p. 24.
[18] See my *Studies in Zen* (London, Rider, 1955), pp. 80 ff.

deeply buried under the bedrock of our being. To split it open requires the most basic tremor of the will. When this is felt the doors of perception open and a new vista hitherto undreamed of is presented. The intellect proposes, and what disposes is not the proposer himself. Whatever we may say about the intellect, it is after all superficial, it is something floating on the surface of consciousness. The surface must be broken through in order to reach the unconscious. But as long as this unconscious belongs in the domain of psychology, there cannot be any *satori* in the Zen sense. The psychology must be transcended and what may be termed the "ontological un-conscious" must be tapped.

The Sung masters must have realized this in their long ex-perience and also in the treatment of their disciples. They wished to break up the intellectual aporia by means of the *"Mu!"* in which there is no trace of intellection but only of the sheer will overriding the intellect. But I must remind my readers not to take me for an anti-intellectualist through and through. What I object to is regarding the intellect as the ultimate reality itself. The intellect is needed to determine, however vaguely, where the reality is. And the reality is grasped only when the intellect quits its claim on it. Zen knows this and proposes as a koan a statement having some savor of intellection, something which in disguise looks as if it de-manded a logical treatment, or rather looks as if there were· room for such treatment. The following examples will demon-strate what I mean:

Yenō, the Sixth Patriarch, is reported to have demanded of his questioner: "Show me your original face you have before you were born." Nangaku Yejō, one of Yenō's disciples, asked one who wanted to be enlightened, "Who is the one who thus comes to me?" One of the Sung masters wanted to know, "Where do we meet after you are dead, cremated, and the ashes are all scattered around?" Hakuin, a great Zen master of modern Japan, used to raise one of his hands before his followers, de-manding, "Let me hear the sound of one hand clapping." There are in Zen many such impossible demands: "Use your spade which is in your empty hands." "Walk while riding on a donkey." "Talk without using your tongue." "Play your stringless lute." "Stop this drenching rain." These paradoxical propositions will no doubt tax one's intellect to the highest degree of tension, finally making him characterize them all as utterly nonsensical and not worth wasting his mental energy on. But nobody will deny the rationality of the following question which has puzzled philosophers, poets, and thinkers of every description ever since the awakening of human consciousness. "Whence do we come and whither do we go?" All those "impossible" questions or statements given out by the Zen masters are no more than "illogical" varieties of the most "rational" question just cited.

As a matter of fact, when you present your logical views of a koan, the master is sure to reject them, categorically or even sarcastically, without giving any ground whatever for doing so. After a few interviews you may not know what to do unless you give him up as "an ignorant old bigot" or as "one who knows nothing of the 'modern rationalistic way' of thinking." But the truth is that the Zen master knows his business much better than you judge. For Zen is not, after all, an intellectual or dialectical game of any sort. It deals with something going beyond the logicalness of things, where he knows there is "the truth that makes one free."

Whatever statement one may make on any subject, it is ineluctably on the surface of consciousness as long as it is amenable in some way to a logical treatment. The intellect serves varied purposes in our daily living, even to the point of annihilating humanity, individually or en masse. No doubt it is a most useful thing, but it does not solve the ultimate problem every one of us sooner or later encounters in the course of his life. This is the problem of life and death, which concerns the meaning of life. When we face it, the intellect has to confess its inability to cope with the problem; for it most certainly comes to an impasse or aporia which in its nature it cannot avoid. The intellectual blind alley to which we are now driven is like "the silver mountain" or "the iron wall" standing right in front of us. Not the intellectual maneuver or logical trickery, but the whole of our being is needed to effect a penetration. It is, the Zen master would tell us, like climbing up to the end of a pole one hundred feet long and yet being urged to climb on and on until you have to execute a desperate leap, utterly disregarding your existential safety. The moment this is executed you find yourself safely on the "full-blown lotus pedestal." This kind of leap can never be attempted by intellection or by logicalness of things. The latter espouses only continuity and never a leap over the gaping chasm. And this is what Zen expects every one of us to accomplish in spite of an apparently logical impossibility. For this reason, Zen always pokes us from behind to go on with our habit of rationalizing in order to make us see by ourselves how far we can go in this futile attempt. Zen knows perfectly well where its limit lies. But we are generally unaware of this fact until we find ourselves at a dead end. This personal experience is needed to wake up the totality of our being, as we are ordinarily too easily satisfied with our intellectual achievements, which are, after all, concerned with life's periphery.

It was not his philosophical training or his ascetic or moral austerities that finally brought Buddha to his experience of enlightenment. Buddha attained it only when he gave up all these superficial practices which hang around the externalities of our existence. Intellection or moralization or conceptualization are only needed to realize their own limitations. The koan exercise aims at bringing all this intimately home to us.

The will in its primary sense, as I said before, is more basic than the intellect because it is the principle that lies at the root of all existences and unites them all in the oneness of being. The rocks are where they are—this is their will. The rivers flow—this is their will. The plants grow—this is their will. The birds fly—this is their will. Human beings talk—this is their will. The seasons change, heaven sends down rain or snow, the earth occasionally shakes, the waves roll, the stars shine—each of them follows its own will. To be is to will and so is to become. There is absolutely nothing in this world that has not its will. The one great will from which all these wills, infinitely varied, flow is what I call the "Cosmic (or ontological) Unconscious," which is the zero-reservoir of infinite possibilities. The *"Mu!"* thus is linked to the unconscious by working on the conative plane of consciousness. The koan that looks intellectual or dialectical, too, finally leads one psychologically to the conative center of consciousness and then to the Source itself.

5.

As I said before, the Zen student, after staying with the master for a few years—no, even a few months—will come to a state of complete standstill. For he does not know which way to go; he has tried to solve the koan on the relative level but to no avail whatever. He is now pushed to the corner where there is no way to escape. At this moment the master may say, "It is good thus to be cornered. The time has come for you to make a complete about-face." The master is likely to continue, "You must not think with the head but with the abdomen, with the belly."

This may sound very strange. According to modern science, the head is filled with masses in gray and white and with cells and fibers connected this way and that. How can the Zen master ignore this fact and advise us to think with the abdomen? But the Zen master is a strange sort of man. He will not listen to you and to what you may tell him about sciences modern or ancient. He knows his business better from his experience.

I have my way of explaining the situation, though perhaps unscientifically. The body may be divided into three parts, that is, functionally: the head, the abdominal parts, and the limbs. The limbs are for locomotion, but the hands have differentiated themselves and developed in their own way. They are now for works of creativity. These two hands with their ten fingers shape all kinds of things meant for the well-being of the body. My intuition is that the hands developed first and then the head, which gradually became an independent organ of thought. When the hands are used this way or that way, they must detach themselves from the ground, differentiating themselves from those of the lower animals. When the human hands are thus freed from the ground, leaving the legs exclusively for locomotion, the hands can follow their own line of development, which will in turn keep the head erect and enable the eyes to survey the more expanding surroundings. The eye is an intellectual organ, while the ear is a more primitive one. As to the nose, it is best for it to keep itself away from the earth, for the eye has now begun to take in a wider horizon. This widening of the visionary field means that the mind becomes more and more detached from sense-objects, making itself an organ of intellectual abstraction and generalization.

Thus the head symbolizes intellection, and the eye, with its mobile muscles, is its useful instrument. But the abdominal part where the viscera are contained is controlled by the involuntary nerves and represents the most primitive stage of evolution in the structure of the human body. The abdominal parts are closer to nature, from which we all come and to which we all return. They are therefore in a more intimate contact with nature and can feel it and talk with it and hold it for "inspection." The inspection, however, is not an intellectual operation; it is, if I can say so, affective. "Feeling" may be a better word when the term is used in its fundamental sense.

Intellectual inspection is the function of the head and therefore whatever understanding we may have of nature from this source is an abstraction or a representation of nature and not nature itself. Nature does not reveal itself as it is to the intellect—that is, to the head. It is the abdominal parts that feel nature and understand it in its suchness. The kind of understanding, which may be called affective or conative, involves the whole being of a person as symbolized by the abdominal parts of the body. When the Zen master tells us to hold the koan in the abdomen, he means that the koan is to be taken up by one's whole being, that one has to identify oneself completely with it, not to look at it intellectually or objectively as if it were something we can stand away from.

Some primitive people were once visited by an American scientist, and when they were told that Western people think with their heads, the primitive people thought that the Americans were all crazy. They said, "We think with the abdomen." People in China and also in Japan—I do not know about India —when some difficult problems come up, often say, "Think with your abdomen," or simply, "Ask your belly." So, when any question in connection with our existence comes up, we are advised to "think" with the belly—not with any detachable part of the body. "The belly" stands for the totality of one's being, while the head, which is the latest-developed portion of the body, represents intellection. The intellect essentially serves us in objectifying the subject under consideration. Therefore, in China especially, the ideal person is one rather corpulent in form, with a protruding abdomen, as is depicted in the figure of Hotei (Pu-tai in Chinese), who is considered an incarnation of the coming Buddha, Maitreya.[19]

To "think" with the abdomen in actuality means to hold the diaphragm down to make room for the thoracic organs to function properly and to keep the body steady and well adjusted for the reception of the koan. The whole procedure is not to make the koan an object of intellection; for the intellect always keeps its object away from itself, to look at it from a distance, as if it were mortally afraid of touching it, not to say anything about grasping and holding it in its own naked hands. Zen, on the contrary, tells us not only to grasp the koan with the hands, with the abdomen, but to identify ourselves with it in a most complete manner, so that when I eat or drink it is not *I* but the koan who eats or drinks. When this is attained the koan solves itself without my doing anything further.

As to the significance of the diaphragm in the structure of the human body I have no knowledge whatever from the medical point of view, but my commonsensical understanding, based on certain experiences, is that the diaphragm in connection with the abdominal part has a great deal to do with one's sense of security, which comes from being more intimately related to the ground of things; that is, to the ultimate reality. To establish this kind of relationship is called in Japanese *kufū suru*. When the Zen master tells you to carry on your *kufū* on the koan with your abdominal part, he means no other act than the attempt at a successful establishment of this relationship. It is perhaps a primitive or ante-scientific way of talking—this way of trying to establish a relationship between the diaphragm and abdomen and the ultimate reality. But there is no doubt, on the other hand, that we have become too nervous about the head and its importance in regard to our intellectual activities. At all events the koan is not to be solved with the head; that is to say, intellectually or philosophically. Whatever logical approach may seem desirable or possible in

---

[19] See my *Manual of Zen Buddhism* (London, Rider, 1950), plate 11, facing p. 129, where the ideal Zen-man comes out to the market—that is, into the world, to save all beings.

the beginning, the koan is destined to be finally settled with the abdominal parts.

Take the case of the staff in the hands of the master. He holds it up and declares, "I do not call it a staff and what would you call it?" This may look as if it required a dialectical answer, for the declaration or challenge is tantamount to saying, "When A is not A, what is it?" or "When God is not God, what is he?" The logical law of identity is here violated. When A is once defined as A, it must remain A and never not-A or B or X. The master would sometimes make another announcement: "The staff is not a staff and yet it is a staff." When the disciple approaches the master logical-mindedly and pronounces the challenge altogether nonsensical, he is sure to be visited with a blow of the very staff in the hands of the master. The disciple cannot escape being driven into an impasse, for the master is adamant and absolutely refuses to yield to any amount of intellectual pressure. Whatever *kufū* the disciple is now compelled to make is all to be carried in his abdominal parts and not in his head. The intellect is to give its place to the will.

To give another example. The Sixth Patriarch demanded to see "the face which you have before your birth." Dialectic is of no avail here. The demand corresponds to Christ's dictum, "I am before Abraham was." Whatever its traditional interpretation on the part of the Christian theologian may be, Christ's *is*-ness defies our human sense of serial time. So with the Sixth Patriarch's "face." The intellect may try all that it can, but the patriarch as well as Christ will most certainly reject it as irrelevant. The head is now to bow to the diaphragm and the mind to the soul. Logic as well as psychology is to be dethroned, to be placed beyond all kinds of intellectualization.

To continue this symbolical talk: The head is conscious while the abdomen is unconscious. When the master tells his disciples to "think" with the lower part of the body, he means that the koan is to be taken down to the unconscious and not to the conscious field of consciousness. The koan is to "sink" into the whole being and not stop at the periphery. Literally, this makes no sense, which goes without saying. But when we realize that the bottom of the unconscious where the koan "sinks" is where even the *ālaya-vijñāna*, "the all-conserving consciousness," [20] cannot hold it, we see that the koan is no more in the field of intellection, it is thoroughly identified with one's Self. The koan is now beyond all the limits of psychology.

When all these limits are transcended—which means going even beyond the so-called collective unconscious—one comes upon what is known in Buddhism as *ādarśanajñāna*, "mirror knowledge." The darkness of the unconscious is broken through and one sees all things as one sees one's face in the brightly shining mirror.

6.

The koan method of studying Zen, as I said before, started in China in the twelfth century with the Sung masters, such as Goso Hōyen (died 1104), Yengo Kokugon (1063-1135), and Daiye Sōkō (1089-1163). But its systematization took place in Japan soon after the introduction of Zen in the thirteenth century. In the beginning the koan was classified under three headings: *prajñā*-intuitional *(richi)*, actional *(kikwan)*, and the ultimate *(kōjō)*. Later, in the seventeenth century, Hakuin and his followers amplified them into five or six, but in essence the older three still hold good. Since, however, the schema was completed, all the Zen students belonging to the Rinzai school nowadays study Zen after it, and the study is more or less stereotyped and to that extent shows signs of deterioration.

The typical and classical examples of the koan students are supplied by Bukkō Kokushi (1226-86) in China and by Hakuin (1685-1768) in Japan.[21] The approach to Zen by those of non-koan system is exemplified, as far as we have the record, by Rinzai (d. 867) in China and by Bankei (1622-93) in Japan.[22]

[20] See *The Lankāvatāra Sūtra* (London, Routledge, 1932), pp. 38, 40, 49, etc., and also my *Essays in Zen Buddhism,* Series 3 (London, Rider, 1951), p. 314.

[21] See my *Essays in Zen Buddhism,* Series 1 (London, Rider, 1949), p. 253 ff, and 252.

[22] Rinzai's *Sayings (Rinzai Roku)*, compiled by his disciples, contains about 13,380 characters and is considered one of the best collections of Zen sayings, known as *Goroku*. The Sung edition of the text which appeared in 1120 is said to be a second one based on a much earlier edition which is however now lost. See my *Studies in Zen,* pp. 25 ff.

For Bankei, see my *Living by Zen,* pp. 11 ff. He was a strong opponent of the koan way of studying Zen which prevailed in his day. He was an elder contemporary of Hakuin, who knew nothing of him as far as we know.

Scholars interested in the further psychological study of Zen are advised to peruse some of my works on the subject.

I would add a few words here. *Jñāna* is ordinarily translated as "knowledge," but to be exact "intuition" may be better. I sometimes translate it "transcendental wisdom," especially when it is prefixed with *pra,* as *prajñā.* The fact is, even when we have an intuition, the object is still in front of us and we sense it, or perceive it, or see it. Here is a dichotomy of subject and object. In *prajñā* this dichotomy no longer exists. *Prajñā* is not concerned with finite objects as such; it is the totality of things becoming conscious of itself as such. And this totality is not at all limited. An infinite totality is beyond our ordinary human comprehension. But the *prajñā*-intuition is this "incomprehensible" totalistic intuition of the infinite, which is something that can never take place in our daily experience limited to finite objects or events. The *prajñā,* therefore, can take place, in other words, only when finite objects of sense and intellect are identified with the infinite itself. Instead of saying that the infinite sees itself in itself, it is much closer to our human experience to say that an object regarded as finite, as belonging in the dichotomous world of subject and object, is perceived by *prajñā* from the point of view of infinity. Symbolically, the finite then sees itself reflected in the mirror of infinity. The intellect informs us that the object is finite, but *prajñā* contradicts, declaring it to be the infinite beyond the realm of relativity. Ontologically, this means that all finite objects or beings are possible because of the infinite underlying them, or that the objects are relatively and therefore limitedly laid out in the field of infinity without which they have no moorings.

This reminds us of St. Paul's epistle to the Corinthians (I Corinthians 13: 12) in which he says: [23] "At present, we are looking at a confused reflection in a mirror; then, we shall see face to face; now, I have only glimpses of knowledge; then I shall recognize God as he has recognized me." "At present" or "now" refers to relative and finite time-sequence, while "then" is eternity, which, in my terminology, is *prajñā*-intuition. In *prajñā*-intuition or "knowledge" I see God as he is in himself,

[23] The Knox version.

not his "confused reflection" or fragmentary "glimpses" of him, because I stand before him "face to face"—no, because I am as he is.

The *ādarśanajñāna* which reveals itself when the bottom of the unconscious, that is, of the *ālaya-vijñāna,* is broken through, is no other than *prajñā*-intuition. The primary will out of which all beings come is not blind and unconscious; it seems so because of our ignorance *(avidyā)* which obscures the mirror, making us oblivious even of the fact of its existence. The blindness is on our side and not on the side of the will, which is primarily and fundamentally noetic as much as conative. The will is *prajñā* plus *karuṇā,* wisdom plus love. On the relative, limited, finite plane, the will is seen as revealed fragmentally; that is to say, we are apt to take it as something separated from our mind-activities. But when it reveals itself in the mirror of *ādarśanajñāna,* it is "God as he is." In him *prajñā* is not differentiated from *karuṇā.* When one is mentioned, the other inevitably comes along.

I cannot help adding another word or two here. An interpersonal relationship is sometimes spoken of in connection with the koan exercise when the master asks a question and the pupil takes it up in his interview with the master. Especially when the master stands rigidly and irrevocably against the pupil's intellectual approach, the pupil, failing to find what to make of the situation, feels as if he were utterly depending on the master's helping hand to pick him up. In Zen this kind of relationship between master and pupil is rejected as not conducive to the enlightenment experience on the part of the pupil. For it is the koan *"Mu!"*, symbolizing the ultimate reality itself, and not the master, that will rise out of the pupil's unconscious. It is the koan *"Mu!"* that makes master knock down pupil, who, when awakened, in turn slaps master's face. There is no Self in its limited finite phase in this wrestlers-like encounter. It is most important that this be unmistakably understood in the study of Zen.

V. THE FIVE STEPS (GO-I)

1.

A number of questions [24] were submitted to me—questions rising out of earlier sessions of this "workshop"—and as I went over them I discovered that most of them seemed to miss the central or pivotal point around which Zen moves. This made me decide today to say something further about Zen life and teaching.

[24] 1. How is it that in the writings of Zen there is so little explicit concern expressed about cultural conditions, the organization of society, and the welfare of man? Associated with this question is the use of Zen (to find oneself ultimately) in the cause of death, as in swordsmanship.

Is there then in such a return to the self some danger of desensitization to the preciousness of every man? Do Zen masters and students participate in the social problems of the day?

2. What is Zen's attitude toward ethics? Toward political and economic deprivation? Toward the individual's position and responsibility toward his society?

3. What is the difference between *satori* and Christian conversion? In one of your books you say you think they are different. Is there any difference other than cultural differences in the ways of talking about it?

4. Christian mysticism is full of erotic images—is there any trace of that in *satori?* Or perhaps in the preceding stages of *satori?*

5. Does Zen have a criterion for differentiating genuine mystic experiences from hallucinatory ones?

6. What interest has Zen in the history of the individual, the influences of family, education, and social institutions in the development of the individual's alienation from himself? Some of us have been interested in this in relation to *prevention* of alienation in the new generations by improvement in individual upbringing as well as social institutions. If we know what determines ill health, presumably we can do something about it before the adult crisis.

7. Does Zen give any thought to the kinds of developmental experiences in childhood that are most conducive to Enlightenment in adulthood?

8. In Zen the master seems to begin with the student without paying attention to the sense of him as he is, or at least he does not react to this explicitly and directly. Yet it is conceivable that such a man might be entering Zen out of vanity or a need to find a new God—of which he may be unconscious. Would it help him find the path if he were in touch with the truth of the fact that his own direction will only turn the experience to ashes?

Does a Zen master communicate his sense of the person and of the obstacles that might be in the way? Even if this does not tend to be done, is it conceivable that if it were done it might make it easier to reach the goal?

9. Do you feel that psychoanalysis, as you understand it, offers patients hope of Enlightenment?

10. What is the attitude of Zen toward images which might appear in the process of meditation?

11. Is Zen concerned with the problem of emotional maturity and self-fulfillment in man's *social* existence, *i.e.,* "interpersonal relationships"?

Zen, we may say, is a strange subject about which we can write or talk for an indefinitely long time, and yet we cannot exhaust all its contents. On the other hand, if we so desired, we could demonstrate it by lifting one finger or by coughing or by winking the eyes or by uttering a meaningless sound.

So it has been stated that even if all the oceans on earth were made into ink, all the mountains into a brush, and the entire world changed into sheets of paper, and we were asked to write on Zen, Zen could not be given full expression. No wonder my short tongue, quite different from Buddha's, fail to make people come to an understanding of Zen in the preceding four lectures.

The following tabular presentation of five "steps," known as *go-i*, in Zen training will facilitate our understanding of Zen. The *"go"* in *go-i* means "five" and the *"i"* means "a situation" or "a rung" or "step." These five are divisible into two groups: noetic, and affective or conative. The first three are noetic and the last two are affective or conative. The middle one, the third "step," is the transition point at which the noetic begins to be conative and knowledge turns into life. Here the noetic comprehension of the Zen life becomes dynamic. "The word" takes flesh; the abstract idea is transformed into a living person who feels, wills, hopes, aspires, suffers, and is capable of doing any amount of work.

In the first of the last two "steps," the Zen-man strives to realize his insight to the utmost of his abilities. In the last he reaches his destination, which is really no destination.

The *go-i* is read in Japanese as follows:
1. *Shō chū hen,* "the *hen* in the *shō*."
2. *Hen chū shō,* "the *shō* in the *hen*."
3. *Shō chū rai,* "the coming from the *shō*."
4. *Ken chū shi,* "the arriving in the *ken*."
5. *Ken chū tō,* "the settling in the *ken*."

The *shō* and the *hen* constitute a duality like the *yin* and *yang* in Chinese philosophy. *Shō* literally means "right," "straight," "just," "level"; and *hen* is "partial," "one-sided," "unbalanced," "lopsided." The English equivalents will be something like these:

The *Shō*	The *Hen*
The absolute	The relative
The infinite	The finite
The one	The many
God	The world
Dark (undifferentiation)	Light (differentiated)
Sameness	Difference
Emptiness *(śūnyatā)*	Form and matter *(nāmarūpa)*
Wisdom *(prajñā)*	Love *(karunā)*
Ri (li) "the universal"	*Ji (shih)* "the particular"

(Let "A" stand for *shō* and "B" for *hen*.

(1) *Shō chū hen,* "the *hen* in the *shō*," means that the one is in the many, God in the world, the infinite in the finite, etc. When we *think,* the *shō* and the *hen* stand in opposition and cannot be reconciled. But in fact the *shō* cannot be the *shō* nor can the *hen* be the *hen* when either stands by itself. What makes the many *(hen)* the many is because the one is in it. If the one is not there, we cannot even talk of manyness.

(2) *Hen chū shō,* "the *shō* in the *hen*," complements (1). If the one is in the many, the many must be in the one. The many is what makes the one possible. God is the world and the world is in God. God and the world are separate and not identical in the sense that God cannot exist outside the world and that the one is indistinguishable from the other. They are one and yet each retains its individuality: God is infinitely particularizing and the world of particulars finds itself nestled in the bosom of God.

(3) We now come to the third step in the life of the Zen-man. This is the most crucial point where the noetic quality of the preceding two steps transforms itself into the conative and he becomes really a living, feeling, and willing personality. Hitherto he was the head, the intellect, in however exacting a sense this might be understood. Now he is supplied with the trunk with all its visceral contents and also with all the limbs, especially with hands, the number of which may be increased even up to one thousand (symbolizing an infinity) like those of

Kwannon the Bodhisattva. And in his inward life he feels like the infant Buddha who uttered, as soon as he came out of his mother's body, this pronouncement: "Heaven above, earth below, I alone am the most honored one."

Incidentally, when I quote this utterance of the Buddha, scientifically minded people may smile and say: "What nonsense! How could a baby fresh from its mother's body make such a deeply philosophical statement? Utterly incredible!" I think they are in the right. But we must remember that while we are rational beings, I hope, at the same time we are the most irrational creatures, fond of all kinds of absurdities called miracles. Did not Christ rise from death and ascend to heaven, though we do not know what sort of heaven that was? Did not his mother, the Virgin Mary, even while alive perform the same wonder? Reason tells us one thing, but there is something besides reason in every one of us and we readily accept miracles. In fact, we, the most commonplace sort of humanity, are also performing miracles at every moment of our lives, regardless of our religious divergencies.

It was Luther who said, "Here I stand, I cannot do otherwise." It was Hyakujo who, when asked what was the most wonderful thing, replied, "I sit alone on the peak of Mount Daiyu." Mount Daiyu is where his monastery was located. In the Chinese original no reference is made to anything or anybody who is sitting; it is just "Alone sit Daiyu Mount." The sitter is not discriminated from the mountain. The aloneness of the Zen-man, in spite of his being in a world of multitudes, is remarkable.

Rinzai's "true man of no title" is no other than the one who is at this moment in front of every one of us, most assuredly listening to my voice as I talk or my word as I write. Is this not the most wonderful fact we all experience? Hence the philosopher's sense of "the mystery of being," if he has actually sensed it.

We ordinarily talk of "I," but "I" is just a pronoun and is not the reality itself. I often feel like asking, "What does 'I' stand for? As long as 'I' is a pronoun like 'you' or 'he' or 'she' or 'it,' what is that which stands behind it? Can you pick it out and tell me, 'This is it'?" The psychologist informs us that "I" is nonexistent, that it is a mere concept designating a structure or an integration of relationships. But the strange fact is that when the "I" gets angry, it wants to destroy the whole world, together with the structure itself for which it is the symbol. Where does a mere concept derive its dynamics? What makes the "I" declare itself to be the only real thing in existence? The "I" cannot just be an allusion or a delusion, it must be something more real and substantial. And it is really real and substantial, because it is "here" where the *shō* and the *hen* are unified as a living identity of the contradiction. All the power "I" has comes from this identity. According to Meister Eckhart, the flea in God is more real than the angel in his own right. The delusive "I" can never be "the most honored one."

The *shō* in *shō chū rai* is not used in the same sense as in *shō chū hen* or in *hen chū shō*. The *shō* in *Shō chū rai* is to be read together with the following *chū* as *shō chū*, meaning "right from the midst of *shō* as *hen* and *hen* as *shō*." *Rai* is "to come," or "to come out." Therefore, the whole combination, *shō chū rai*, means "the one as coming right from the midst of *shō* and *hen* in their contradictory identity."

If we establish the following formulas where *shō* is A and *hen* is B, the first step is

and the second is

The third then will be

But as the third signifies the turning point of the noetic into the conative and of logic into personality, it is to be formulated in the following way:

That is to say, each straight line is to change into a curve indicating movement; and we must remember that, as this movement is not a mere mechanical thing but is living, creative, and inexhaustible, the curved arrow is not enough. Perhaps we might set the whole symbol in a circle, making it represent a *dharmacakra*, the cosmic wheel in its never-ending revolution, thus:

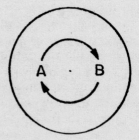

Or we may adapt the Chinese symbol of their *yin* and *yang* philosophy as a symbol of the *Shō chū rai:*

Rai in *shō chū rai* is significant. Movement is indicated here, together with *shi* in the fourth step, *ken chū shi. Rai* is "to come out," and *shi* means "in the process of reaching the destination," or "to be moving toward the goal." The logical abstraction, Logos, now steps out of its cage and becomes incarnated, personalized, and walks right into a world of complexities like "the golden-haired lion."

This "golden-haired lion" is the "I" who is at once finite and infinite, transient and permanent, limited and free, absolute and relative. This living figure reminds me of Michelangelo's famous "Christ on Judgment Day," a fresco in the Sistine Chapel. But the Zen "I," as far as its outward manifestations go, is not at all like the Christ, so energetic and power-wielding and commanding. He is meek, unobtrusive, and full of humility.

Some philosophers and theologians talk about the Oriental "Silence" in contrast to the Western "Word" which becomes the "flesh." They do not, however, understand what the East really means by "silence," for it does not stand against the "word," it is the word itself, it is the "thunderous silence" and not the one sinking into the depths of non-entity, nor is it one absorbed in the eternal indifference of death. The Eastern silence resembles the eye of a hurricane; it is the center of the raging storm and without it no motion is possible. To extract this center of immobility from its surroundings is to conceptualize it and to destroy its meaning. The eye is what makes the hurricane possible. Eye and hurricane conjointly constitute the totality. The quietly floating duck on the surface of the lake is not to be separated from its legs most busily moving, though unseen, under the water. Dualists generally miss the whole in its coherent concrete totality.

Those who think dualistically are apt one-sidedly to emphasize the motile aspect or the visible fleshy aspect of reality and, ignoring everything else, to attach to it the greatest importance. For instance, ballet dancing is characteristically a product of the West. Rhythmical movement of the body and the limbs go on most briskly in all their harmonious complexities. Compare them with the Japanese *nō* dance. What a contrast! The ballet is almost movement itself, with the feet hardly touching the ground. The movement is in the air; stability is conspicuously absent. In *nō* the stage presents quite a different spectacle. Steadily, solemnly, as if performing a religious rite, keeping his feet solidly on the ground and his center of gravity in the abdominal parts of his body, the actor steps out from the *hanamichi* to the expectant gaze of the audience. He moves as if not moving. He illustrates the Lao-tsean doctrine of the action of nonaction.

In a similar way the Zen-man is never obtrusive, but always self-effacing and altogether unassuming. While he declares himself to be "the most honored one," there is nothing in his outward mien exhibiting his inner life. He is the unmoved mover. This is, indeed, where the real "I" emerges, not the "I" each one of us ordinarily asserts, but the "I" discovering itself *sub specie eternitatis,* in the midst of infinity. This "I" is the securest ground which we all can find in ourselves and on which we all can stand without fear, without the sense of anxiety, without the harassing moment of indecision. This "I" is negligible almost to nonexistence because it is not at all pre-suming and never boisterously proclaims itself to be recognized and made most of. Dualists miss this; they exalt the ballet dancer and are bored by the *nō* actor.

When we were discussing Sullivan's idea of anxiety [see Foreword], it developed that anxiety could be of two kinds, neurotic anxiety and existential anxiety, that the latter was more basic, and, further, that when the basic anxiety was solved the neurotic one would be solved by itself. All forms of anxiety come from the fact that there is somewhere in our conscious-ness the feeling of incomplete knowledge of the situation and this lack of knowledge leads to the sense of insecurity and then to anxiety with all its degrees of intensity. The "I" is always at the center of whatever situation we may encounter. When, therefore, the "I" is not thoroughly known, such questions and thoughts as follows never cease to torment us:

"Has life any meaning?"

"Is all really 'vanity of vanities'? If so, is there any hope of taking hold of what it is truly worth while to attain?"

"I am thrown into the whirlpool of brute facts, all given, all limited, all absolutely definitely unchanged, etc. I am helpless; I am the plaything of fates. Yet I long for freedom; I want to be master of myself. I cannot make my choice; yet a decision, one way or another, is imperative. I do not know what to do. But what am 'I' who really stands at the back of all these puzzling and harassing questions?"

"Where then is the secure ground I can stand on without any sense of anxiety? Or, what is 'I'? For I know 'I' may be the secure ground itself. Could this be the fact which I have not been able to discover so far? The 'I' must be discovered. And I shall be all right!"

2.

Shō chū rai has already given the answer to all these thoughts, but when we come to the fourth step, *Ken chū shi*, we shall know more about the "I" in its intense activity, which, however, is no-activity. This will, I hope, become comprehensible when we come to the fifth and last step, where the Zen-man would reach his final goal. He is found there innocently sitting covered with dirt and ashes.

(4) With these remarks let us move on to the fourth step. In fact, the third and the fourth are intimately related and the one cannot be taken up without the other.

Inasmuch as the Zen-man is logically or noetically minded, he is still conscious of the *shō* and the *hen* and may feel like referring to their contradictory identity. But as soon as he steps into the *Ken chū shi*, he is out of the hurricane's eye and has plunged himself into the midst of the storm. Both the *shō* and the *hen* are cast away to the four winds. The man is now the storm itself.

Ken means "both" and refers to the dualism of black and white, dark and light, love and hate, good and bad—which is the actuality of the world in which the Zen-man leads his life now. While *Shō chū rai* still reminds us of something in the preceding two steps, *Ken chū shi* has altogether left them behind, for it is life itself shorn of its intellectual paradoxes, or rather, it includes indiscriminately, undifferentially, or better, totalistically, everything that is intellectual or affective or conative. It is the world as we have it with all its "brute facts," as some philosophers take them, irrevocably facing us. The Zen-man has now "set his feet" *(shi)* right into them. His real life starts here. This is the meaning of *Ken chū shi:* "He has now come into the midst of dualities *(ken)*." Here, really, in all actuality begins the Zen-man's life of love *(karunā)*.

Jōshū Jūshin, one of the great T'ang Zen masters, had his

monastery in the mountains noted for a natural stone bridge. One day a monk visited Jōshū and said: "O Master, your stone bridge is noted all over the empire, but as I see it it is nothing but a rickety log bridge."

Jōshū retorted, "You see your rickety one and fail to see the real stone bridge."

The monk asked, "What is the stone bridge?"

Jōshū: "Horses pass over it; donkeys pass over it."

Jōshū's bridge resembles the sands of the Ganges, which are trampled by all kinds of animals and incredibly soiled by them, and yet the sands make no complaint whatever. All the footprints left by creatures of every description are effaced in no time; and as to their filths, they are all effectively absorbed, leaving the sands as clean as ever. So with Jōshū's stone bridge: not only horses and donkeys but nowadays all kinds of conveyances, including heavy trucks and trains of cars, pass over it and it is ever willing to accommodate them. Even when they abuse it its complacency is not at all disturbed. The Zen-man of the "fourth step" is like the bridge. He may not turn the right cheek to be struck when the left one is already hurt, but he works silently for the welfare of his fellow beings.

Jōshū was once asked by an old woman: "I am a woman and the life of womanhood is very hard. When a child, she suffers to obey her parents. When she is old enough, she marries and has to obey the husband. When she is very old, she obeys her children. Her life is nothing but obeying and obeying. Why is she made to lead such a life with no period of freedom and independence? Why is she not like other people who go even without the sense of responsibility? I revolt against the old Chinese way of living."

Jōshū said, [Let your prayer be:] "others may have all they like. As regards myself, I go on with the lot assigned to me."

Jōshū's advice, one may protest, is no more than a life of absolute dependence, which is not at all the spirit of modern life. His advice is too conservative, too negative, too self-effacing; there is no sense of individuality. Is this not typical of the Buddhist teaching of *khsānti*, passivity, nothingness? I am no advocate of Jōshū.

Let Jōshū answer, in a way, this objection when he expresses his own idea thus:

Someone asked, "You are such a saintly personality. Where would you find yourself after your death?"

Jōshū the Zen master replied, "I go to hell ahead of you all!"

The questioner was thunderstruck and said, "How could that be?"

The master did not hesitate: "Without my first going to hell, who would be waiting there to save people like you?"

This is, indeed, a strong statement, but from Jōshū's Zen point of view he was fully justified. He has no selfish motive here. His whole existence is devoted to doing good for others. If not for this, he could not make such a straightforward statement with no equivocation whatever. Christ declares, "I am the Way." He calls others to be saved through him. Jōshū's spirit is also Christ's. There is no arrogant self-centered spirit in either of them. They simply, innocently, wholeheartedly express the same spirit of love.

Somebody asked Jōshū, "Buddha is the enlightened one and teacher of us all. He is naturally entirely free of all the passions (kleśa), is he not?"

Jōshū said, "No, he is the one who cherishes the greatest of all the passions."

"How is that possible?"

"His greatest passion is to save all beings!" Jōshū answered.

One of the great Zen masters of Japan describes the Zen-man's life at this point as follows: [24]

The bodhisattva would revolve the identity-wheel of opposites or contradictions: black and white, dark and bright, sameness and difference, the one and the many, finite and infinite, love and hate, friend and foe, etc., etc. While in the midst of clouds and dust, infinitely variegated, the bodhisattva works with his head and face all covered with mud and ashes. Where the utmost confusion of passions rages in its indescribable furies, the bodhisattva lives his life in all its vicissitudes, as the Japanese proverb has it, "seven times rolling up and down, and eight times getting up straight." He is like the lotus flower

[24] The wording has been partly modernized.

in flame, whose color grows brighter and brighter as it goes
through the baptism of fire.

The following is the way Rinzai describes his "man of no
title":

He is the one who is in the house and yet does not stay away from
the road, he is the one who is on the road and yet does not stay
away from the house. Is he an ordinary man or a great sage? No
one can tell. Even the devil does not know where to locate him.
Even the Buddha fails to manage him as he may desire. When
we try to point him out, he is no more there, he is on the other
side of the mountain.

In the *Lotus Sūtra* we have this: "As long as there is one
single solitary soul not saved, I am coming back to this world
to help him." In the same sūtra Buddha says: "A bodhisattva
would never enter into final nirvāna. He would stay on among
all beings (*sarvasattva*) and work for their edification and enlightenment. He would see to it that he was not to shun any
amount of suffering if it were at all conducive to the general
welfare."

There is a Mahayana sūtra called the *Yuima-kyō (Vimalakīr-
tisūtra)*, the principal interlocutor here being a lay disciple
of Buddha and a great philosopher. Once he was reported to
be ill. Buddha wanted one of his disciples to go and inquire
after his health. None accepted because Yuima was such an
invincible debater that none of his contemporaries could beat
him. Monju (or Mañjuśrí) was willing to carry out Buddha's
commission.

When Monju asked Yuima about his illness, the latter
answered, "I am ill because all beings are ill. My illness is
curable only when they are cured. They are constantly assailed
by Greed, Anger, and Folly."

Love and compassion, we can thus see, are the essence of
Buddahood and bodhisattvaship. These "passions" make
them stay with all beings as long as there is any one of them
still in the state of unenlightenment. A Japanese proverb says:
"To this world of patience they come and go for eight thousand
times," meaning that Buddhas and bodhisattvas would for an
indefinite number of times visit this world of ours, which is

full of unendurable sufferings, just because their love knows no bounds.

One great contribution the Chinese made to Buddhism is their idea of work. The first conscious effort to establish work as an aspect of Buddhism was made about one thousand years ago by Hyakujo, the founder of the Zen monastery system in distinction to other Buddhist institutions. Before Hyakujo the Buddhist monks were devoted chiefly to learning, meditation, and observing the *vinaya* precepts. But Hyakujo was not satisfied with this; he aspired to follow the example of Yenō, the Sixth Patriarch, who was a farmer in southern China and earned his living by cutting wood and selling fuel. When Yeno was allowed to join the brotherhood, he was assigned to the back yard, where he pounded rice, prepared kindling, and performed other menial work.

When Hyakujo organized a new monastery exclusively for Zen monks one of his rules was to work; each monk, including the master himself, was to engage in some manual, menial labor. Even when he was getting old Hyakujo refused to leave off his gardening work. His disciples worried over his advanced age and hid all his garden implements, so that he would no longer work as hard as he used to. But Hyakujo declared, "If I do not work I will not eat."

For this reason, one thing which characterizes the Zen temples and monasteries in Japan, as well as in China, is that they are kept clean and in good order, and the monks are ready to take up any sort of manual labor, however dirty and undesirable it may be.

This spirit of work is perhaps deeply ingrained in Chinese minds since of old, for, as referred to in my first chapter, Chuang-tze's farmer refused to make use of the shadoof and did not mind doing any amount of work just for the love of it. This is not in accord with the Western and, indeed, the modern idea of labor-saving devices of every description. When they have thus saved themselves from labor and gained plenty of time for their pleasures or other employments, modern people are busy making up all sorts of complaints about how dissatisfied they are with life, or inventing weapons whereby they can kill thousands of human beings by simply pressing a button.

And listen to what they say: "This is the way to prepare for peace." Is it not really wonderful to realize that when the fundamental evils lurking in human nature are not destroyed and its intellectuality alone is given free rein to work itself out in the way it likes, it exerts itself to discover the easiest and quickest way of annihilating itself from the surface of the earth? When Chuang-tze's farmer refused to be machine-minded, did he foresee all these evils coming a little over twenty-one or twenty-two centuries after him? Confucius says, "When small men have plenty of time at hand they are sure to devise all kinds of evil things."

Before concluding this, let me give you what may be called the cardinal virtues of the bodhisattva or Zen-man. They are known as the six *pāramitās:*

      i. *Dāna* (charity)
     ii. *Śīla* (precepts)
    iii. *Kṣānti* (humility)
     iv. *Vīrya* (energy)
      v. *Dhyāna* (meditation)
     vi. *Prajñā* (wisdom)

(i) Charity, or giving, is to give away for the benefit and welfare of all beings *(sarvasattva)* anything and everything one is capable of giving: not only material goods, but knowledge, worldly as well as religious or spiritual (knowledge belonging to the Dharma, the ultimate truth). The bodhisattvas were all ready to give up even their lives to save others. (Fantastic stories about the bodhisattvas are told in the *Jataka Tales.)*

The history of Japanese Buddhism gives one conspicuous example of self-sacrifice on the part of a Zen master. It was during the political period known as the Warring Era in the sixteenth century when Japan was torn into a number of independent dukedoms which were controlled by the warring lords. Oda Nobunaga came out the strongest. When he defeated the neighboring Takeda family, one of the latter took refuge in a Zen monastery. The Oda army demanded his surrender into their hands, but the abbot refused, saying, "He is now my protégé and as Buddha's follower I cannot give him up." The besieging general threatened to burn the entire monastery, together with the occupants. As the abbot was still unyielding, the edifice, consisting of several buildings, was put to flame. The abbot, with a few monks who were willing to join him, was driven up to the second floor of the tower gate, where they all sat cross-legged. The abbot, demanding that they express whatever thought they had on this occasion, told his devotees to prepare for the last moment. Each gave his view. When it came to be the abbot's turn he quietly recited the following lines, then was burned alive with the rest:

> For the peaceful practice of *dhyāna* (meditation)
> It's not necessary to go to the mountain retreat.
> Have the mind cleansed of the passions,
> And even the flames are cool and refreshing.

(ii) *Śīla* is observing the precepts, given by Buddha, which are conducive to moral life. In the case of the homeless ones, the precepts are meant to maintain the order of the brotherhood *(sangha)*. The *sangha* is a model society the ideal of which is to lead a peaceful, harmonious life.

(iii) *Kṣānti* is generally understood to mean "patience," but it really means patiently, or rather with equanimity, to go through deeds of humiliation. Or as Confucius says, "The superior man would cherish no ill-feeling even when his work or merit is not recognized by others." No Buddhist devotees would feel humiliated when they were not fully appreciated, no, even when they were unjustly ignored. They would also go on patiently under all unfavorable conditions.

(iv) *Vīrya* etymologically means "virility." It is always to be devoted and energetic in carrying out everything that is in accordance with the Dharma.

(v) *Dhyāna* is retaining one's tranquil state of mind in any circumstance, unfavorable as well as favorable, and not being at all disturbed or frustrated even when adverse situations present themselves one after another. This requires a great deal of training.

(vi) *Prajñā*. There is no corresponding English word, in fact, no European word, for it, for European people have no experience specifically equivalent to *prajñā*. *Prajñā* is the experience a man has when he feels in its most fundamental sense the infinite totality of things, that is, psychologically speaking, when the finite ego, breaking its hard crust, refers itself to the infinite which envelops everything that is finite and limited and therefore transitory. We may take this experience as being somewhat akin to a totalistic intuition of something that transcends all our particularized, specified experiences.

3.

(5) We now come to the last step, *Ken chū tō*. The difference between this and the fourth is the use of *tō* instead of *shi*. *Shi* and *tō* mean, in fact, the same action, "to arrive," "to reach." But according to the traditional interpretation, *shi* has not yet completed the act of reaching, the traveler is still on the way to the goal, whereas *tō* indicates the completion of the act. The Zen-man here attains his object, for he has reached the destination. He is working just as strenuously as ever; he stays in this world among his fellow beings. His daily activities are not changed; what is changed is his subjectivity. Hakuin, the founder of modern Rinzai Zen in Japan, has this to say about it:

> By hiring that idiot-sage,
> Let us work together to fill
> the well with snow.

After all, there is not much to say about the Zen-man's life here, because his outward behavior does not mean much; he is all involved in his inner life. Outwardly he may be in rags and working in the capacity of an insignificant laborer. In feudal Japan, unknown Zen-men were frequently found among the beggars. At least there was one case of this nature. When this man died, his bowl for rice, with which he went around begging food, was accidentally examined and found to have an inscription in classical Chinese that expressed his view of life and his understanding of Zen. In fact, Bankei, the great Zen master, himself was once in the company of the beggars before he was discovered and gave his consent to teach one of the feudal lords of the day.

Before concluding, I will quote one or two *mondō* character-izing Zen and hope they will throw some light on the pre-ceding accounts of the Zen-man's life. Perhaps one of the most noticeable facts in this life is that the notion of love as it is understood by Buddhists lacks the demonstrative feature of eroticism which we observe strongly manifested by some of the Christian saints. Their love is directed in a very special way toward Christ, whereas Buddhists have almost nothing to do with Buddha but with their fellow beings, nonsentient as well as sentient. Their love manifests itself in the form of un-grudged and self-sacrificing labor for others, as we have seen above.

There was an old woman who kept a teahouse at the foot of Mount Taisan, where was located a Zen monastery noted all over China. Whenever a traveling monk asked her which was the way to Taisan, she would say, "Go straight ahead." When the monk followed her direction, she would remark, "Here is another who goes the same way." Zen monks did not know what to make of her remark.

The report reached Jōshū. Jōshū said, "Well, I'll go and see what kind of woman she is." He started and, coming to the teahouse, asked the old lady which road led to Taisan. Sure enough, she told him to go straight ahead, and Jōshū did just as many another monk had done. Remarked the woman, "A fine monk, he goes just the same way as the rest." When Jōshū came back to his brotherhood, he reported, "Today I have found her out through and through!"

We may ask, "What did the old master find in the woman when his behavior was in no way different from that of the rest of the monks?" This is the question each of us has to solve in his own way.

To summarize, what Zen proposes for us to do is: To seek Enlightenment for oneself and to help others attain it. Zen has what may be called "prayers," though they are quite differ-ent from those of Christians. Four are generally enumerated, the last two of which are a kind of amplification of the first two:

i. However numberless all beings be, I pray that they may all be saved.

ii. However inexhaustible the passions be, I pray that they may all be eradicated.

iii. However immeasurably differentiated the Dharma is, I pray that it may all be studied.

iv. However supremely exalted the Buddha-Way may be, I pray that it may all be attained.

Zen may occasionally appear too enigmatic, cryptic, and full of contradictions, but it is after all a simple discipline and teaching:

> To do goods,
> To avoid evils,
> To purify one's own heart:
> This is the Buddha-Way.

Is this not applicable to all human situations, modern as well as ancient, Western as well as Eastern?

PSYCHOANALYSIS
AND ZEN BUDDHISM

by Erich Fromm

In relating Zen Buddhism to psychoanalysis, one discusses two systems, both dealing with a theory concerned with the nature of man and with a practice leading to his well-being. Each is a characteristic expression of Eastern and Western thought, respectively. *Zen Buddhism* is a blending of Indian rationality and abstraction with Chinese concreteness and realism. *Psychoanalysis* is as exquisitely Western as Zen is Eastern; it is the child of Western humanism and rationalism, and of the nineteenth-century romantic search for the dark forces which elude rationalism. Much further back, Greek wisdom and Hebrew ethics are the spiritual godfathers of this scientific-therapeutic approach to man.

But in spite of the fact that both psychoanalysis and Zen deal with the nature of man and with a practice leading to his transformation, the differences seem to outweigh these similarities. Psychoanalysis is a scientific method, nonreligious to its core. Zen is a theory and technique to achieve "enlightenment," an experience which in the West would be called religious or mystical. Psychoanalysis is a therapy for mental illness; Zen a way to spiritual salvation. Can the discussion of the relationship between psychoanalysis and Zen Buddhism result in anything but the statement that there exists no relationship except that of radical and unbridgeable difference?

Yet there is an unmistakable and increasing interest in Zen

Buddhism among psychoanalysts.[1] What are the sources of this interest? What is its meaning? To give an answer to these questions is what this paper attempts to do. It does not try to give a systematic presentation of Zen Buddhist thought, a task which would transcend my knowledge and experience; nor does it try to give a full presentation of psychoanalysis, which would go beyond the scope of this paper. Nevertheless, I shall—in the first part of this paper—present in some detail those aspects of psychoanalysis which are of immediate relevance to the relation between psychoanalysis and Zen Buddhism and which, at the same time, represent basic concepts of that continuation of Freudian analysis which I sometimes have called "humanistic psychoanalysis." I hope in this way to show why the study of Zen Buddhism has been of vital significance to me and, as I believe—is significant for all students of psychoanalysis.

I. TODAY'S SPIRITUAL CRISIS AND THE ROLE OF PSYCHOANALYSIS

As a first approach to our topic, we must consider the spiritual crisis which Western man is undergoing in this crucial historical epoch, and the function of psychoanalysis in this crisis.

While the majority of people living in the West do not consciously feel as if they were living through a crisis of Western culture (probably never have the majority of people in a radically critical situation been aware of the crisis), there is agreement, at least among a number of critical observers, as to the existence and the nature of this crisis. It is the crisis which has been described as "malaise," "ennui," "mal du siècle," the deadening of life, the automatization of man, his alienation

---

[1] Cf. Jung's introduction to D. T. Suzuki's *Zen Buddhism* (London, Rider, 1949); the French psychiatrist Benoit's work on Zen Buddhism, *The Supreme Doctrine* (New York, Pantheon Books, 1955). The late Karen Horney was intensely interested in Zen Buddhism during the last years of her life. The conference held in Cuernavaca, Mexico, at which the papers published in this book were presented, is another symptom of the interest of psychoanalysts in Zen Buddhism. There is also considerable interest in Japan in the relation between psychotherapy and Zen Buddhism. Cf. Koji Sato's paper on "Psychotherapeutic Implications of Zen," in *Psychologia, An International Journal of Psychology in the Orient,* Vol. I, No. 4 (1958), and other papers in the same issue.

from himself, from his fellow man and from nature.[2] Man has followed rationalism to the point where rationalism has transformed itself into utter irrationality. Since Descartes, man has increasingly split thought from affect; thought alone is considered rational—affect, by its very nature, irrational; the person, *I*, has been split off into an intellect, which constitutes my self, and which is to control *me* as it is to control nature. Control by the intellect over nature, and the production of more and more things, became the paramount aims of life. In this process man has transformed himself into a thing, life has become subordinated to property, *"to be"* is dominated by *"to have."* Where the roots of Western culture, both Greek and Hebrew, considered the aim of life the *perfection of man*, modern man is concerned with the *perfection of things*, and the knowledge of how to make them. Western man is in a state of schizoid inability to experience affect, hence he is anxious, depressed, and desperate. He still pays lip service to the aims of happiness, individualism, initiative—but actually he has no aim. Ask him what he is living for, what is the aim of all his strivings—and he will be embarrassed. Some may say they live for the family, others, "to have fun," still others, to make money, but in reality nobody knows what he is living for; he has no goal, except the wish to escape insecurity and aloneness.

It is true, church membership today is higher than ever before, books on religion become best sellers, and more people speak of God than ever before. Yet this kind of religious profession only covers up a profoundly materialistic and irreligious attitude, and is to be understood as an ideological reaction—caused by insecurity and conformism—to the trend of the nineteenth century, which Nietzsche characterized by his famous "God is dead." As a truly religious attitude, it has no reality.

The abandonment of theistic ideas in the nineteenth century was—seen from one angle—no small achievement. Man took a big plunge into objectivity. The earth ceased to be the center of the universe; man lost his central role of the creature destined by God to dominate all other creatures. Studying man's hidden motivations with a new objectivity, Freud recognized that the

---

[2] Cf. the writings of Kierkegaard, Marx, and Nietzsche and, at present, of existentialist philosophers and of Lewis Mumford, Paul Tillich, Erich Kahler, David Riesman, and others.

faith in an all-powerful, omniscient God, had its root in the helplessness of human existence and in man's attempt to cope with his helplessness by means of belief in a helping father and mother represented by God in heaven. He saw that man only can save himself; the teaching of the great teachers, the loving help of parents, friends, and loved ones can help him—but can help him only to dare to accept the challenge of existence and to react to it with all his might and all his heart.

Man gave up the illusion of a fatherly God as a parental helper—but he gave up also the true aims of all great humanistic religions: overcoming the limitations of an egotistical self, achieving love, objectivity, and humility and respecting life so that the aim of life is living itself, and man becomes what he potentially is. These were the aims of the great Western religions, as they were the aims of the great Eastern religions. The East, however, was not burdened with the concept of a transcendent father-savior in which the monotheistic religions expressed their longings. Taoism and Buddhism had a rationality and realism superior to that of the Western religions. They could see man realistically and objectively, having nobody but the "awakened" ones to guide him, and being able to be guided because each man has within himself the capacity to awake and be enlightened. This is precisely the reason why Eastern religious thought, Taoism and Buddhism—and their blending in Zen Buddhism—assume such importance for the West today. Zen Buddhism helps man to find an answer to the question of his existence, an answer which is essentially the same as that given in the Judaeo-Christian tradition, and yet which does not contradict the rationality, realism, and independence which are modern man's precious achievements. Paradoxically, Eastern religious thought turns out to be more congenial to Western rational thought than does Western religious thought itself.

II. VALUES AND GOALS IN FREUD'S PSYCHOANALYTIC CONCEPTS

Psychoanalysis is a characteristic expression of Western man's spiritual crisis, and an attempt to find a solution. This is explicitly so in the more recent developments of psychoanalysis, in "humanist" or "existentialist" analysis. But before I discuss my own "humanist" concept, I want to show that, quite contrary to a widely held assumption Freud's own system transcended the concept of "illness" and "cure" and was concerned with the "salvation" of man, rather than only with a therapy for mentally sick patients. Superficially seen, Freud was the creator of a new therapy for mental illness, and this was the subject matter to which his main interest and all the efforts of his life were devoted. However, if we look more closely, we find that behind this concept of a medical therapy for the cure of neurosis was an entirely different interest, rarely expressed by Freud, and probably rarely conscious even to himself. This hidden or only implicit concept did not primarily deal with the cure of mental illness, but with something which transcended the concept of illness and cure. What was this something? What was the nature of the "psychoanalytic movement" he founded? What was Freud's vision for man's future? What was the dogma on which his movement was founded?

Freud answered this question perhaps most clearly in the sentence: "Where there was Id—there shall be Ego." His aim was the domination of irrational and unconscious passions by reason; the liberation of man from the power of the unconscious, within the possibilities of man. Man had to become aware of the unconscious forces within him, in order to dominate and control them. Freud's aim was the optimum knowledge of truth, and that is the knowledge of reality; this knowledge to him was the only guiding light man had on this earth. These aims were the traditional aims of rationalism, of the Enlightenment philosophy, and of Puritan ethics. But while religion and philosophy had postulated these aims of self-control in what might be called a *utopian* way, Freud was—or believed himself to be—the first one to put these aims on a *scientific* basis (by the exploration of the unconscious) and hence to show the way to their realization. While Freud represents the culmination of Western rationalism, it was his genius to overcome at the same time the false rationalistic and superficially optimistic aspects of rationalism, and to create a synthesis with romanticism, the very movement which during the nineteenth century opposed rationalism by its own interest in and reverence for the irrational, affective side of man.[3]

With regard to the treatment of the individual, Freud was also more concerned with a philosophical and ethical aim than he was generally believed to be. In the Introductory Lectures, he speaks of the attempts certain mystical practices make to produce a basic transformation within the personality. "We have to admit," he continues, "that the therapeutic efforts of psychoanalysis have chosen a similar point of approach. Its intention is to strengthen the Ego, to make it more independent from the Super-Ego, to enlarge its field of observation, so that it can appropriate for itself new parts of the Id. Where there was Id there shall be Ego. It is a work of culture like the reclamation of the Zuyder Zee." In the same vein he speaks of psychoanalytic therapy as consisting in *the liberation of the human being* from his neurotic symptoms, inhibitions and abnormalities of character." [4] He sees also the role of the analyst in a light which transcends that of the doctor who "cures" the patient. "The analyst," he says, "must be in a superior position in some sense, if he is to serve as a *model* for the patient in certain analytic situations, and in others to act as his *teacher*." [5] "Finally," Freud writes, "we must not forget that the relationship between analyst and patient is based on a *love of truth*, that is, on acknowledgment of reality, that it precludes any kind of *sham*, and *deception*." [6]

There are other factors in Freud's concept of psychoanalysis which transcend the conventional notion of illness and cure. Those familiar with Eastern thought, and especially with Zen Buddhism, will notice that the factors which I am going to mention are not without relation to concepts and thoughts of the Eastern mind. The principle to be mentioned here first is Freud's concept that *knowledge leads to transformation,* that theory and practice must not be separated, that in the very act of *knowing* oneself, one *transforms* oneself. It is hardly neces-

[3] For details of the quasi-religious character of the psychoanalytic movement which Freud created, cf. my *Sigmund Freud's Mission,* World Perspective Series, ed. R. N. Anshen (New York, Harper, 1959).

[4] "Analysis Terminable and Unterminable," *Collected Papers,* Hogarth Press, V, 316. (Italics mine—E. F.)

[5] *Ibid.,* p. 351. (Italics mine—E. F.)

[6] *Ibid.,* p. 352. (Italics mine—E. F.)

sary to emphasize how different this idea is from the concepts of scientific psychology in Freud's or in our time, where knowledge in itself remains theoretical knowledge, and has not a transforming function in the knower.

In still another aspect Freud's method has a close connection with Eastern thought, and especially with Zen Buddhism. Freud did not share the high evaluation of our conscious thought system, so characteristic of modern Western man. On the contrary, he believed that our conscious thought was only a small part of the whole of the psychic process going on in us and, in fact, an insignificant one in comparison with the tremendous power of those sources within ourselves which are dark and irrational and at the same time unconscious. Freud, in his wish to arrive at insight into the real nature of a person, wanted to break through the conscious thought system, by his method of *free association*. Free association was to by-pass logical, conscious, conventional thought. It was to lead into a new source of our personality, namely, the unconscious. Whatever criticism may be made of the *contents* of Freud's unconscious, the fact remains that by emphasizing free association as against logical thought, he transcended in an essential point the conventional rationalistic mode of thinking of the Western world, and moved in a direction which had been developed much farther and much more radically in the thought of the East.

There is one further point in which Freud differs radically from the contemporary Western attitude. I refer here to the fact that he was willing to analyze a person for one, two, three, four, five, or even more years. This procedure has, in fact, been the reason for a great deal of criticism against Freud. Needless to say, one should attempt to make analysis as efficient as possible, but the point I mean to stress here is that Freud had the courage to say that one could meaningfully spend years with one person, just to help this person to understand himself. From a standpoint of utility, from a standpoint of loss and profit, this does not make too much sense. One would rather say that the time spent in such a prolonged analysis is not worth while, if one considers the *social effect* of a change in one person. Freud's method makes sense only if one transcends the modern concept of "value," of the proper relationship between means and ends, of the balance sheet, as it were; if one takes the position that one human being is not commensurable with any *thing,* that his emancipation, his well-being, his enlightenment, or whatever term we might want to use, is a matter of "ultimate concern" in itself, then no amount of time and money can be related to this aim in quantitative terms. To have had the vision and the courage to devise a method which implied this extended concern with one person was a manifestation of an attitude which transcended Western conventional thought in an important aspect.

The foregoing remarks are not meant to imply that Freud, in his conscious intentions, was close to Eastern thought or specifically to the thought of Zen Buddhism. Many of the elements which I mentioned before were more implicit than explicit, and more unconscious than conscious, in Freud's own mind. Freud was much too much a son of Western civilization, and especially of eighteenth- and nineteenth-century thought, to be close to Eastern thought as expressed in Zen Buddhism, even if he had been familiar with it. Freud's picture of man was in essential features the picture which the economists and philosophers of the eighteenth and nineteenth centuries had developed. They saw man as essentially competitive, isolated, and related to others only by the necessity of exchanging the satisfaction of economic and instinctual needs. For Freud, man is a machine, driven by the libido, and regulated by the principle of keeping libido excitation to a minimum. He saw man as fundamentally egotistical, and related to others only by the mutual necessity of satisfying instinctual desires. Pleasure, for Freud, was relief of tension, not the experience of joy. Man was seen split between his intellect and his affects; man was not the whole man, but the intellect-self of the Enlightenment philosophers. Brotherly love was an unreasonable demand, contrary to reality; mystical experience a regression to infantile narcissism.

What I have tried to show is that in spite of these obvious contradictions to Zen Buddhism, there were nevertheless elements in Freud's system which transcended the conventional concepts of illness and cure, and the traditional rationalistic concepts of consciousness, elements which led to a further development of psychoanalysis which has a more direct and positive affinity with Zen Buddhist thought.

However, before we come to the discussion of the connection between this "humanistic" psychoanalysis and Zen Buddhism, I want to point to a change which is fundamental for the understanding of the further development of psychoanalysis: the change in the kinds of patients who come for analysis, and the problems they present.

At the beginning of this century the people who came to the psychiatrist were mainly people who suffered from *symptoms*. They had a paralyzed arm, or an obsessional symptom like a washing compulsion, or they suffered from obsessional thoughts which they could not get rid of. In other words, they were sick in the sense in which the word "sickness" is used in medicine; something prevented them from functioning socially as the so-called normal person functions. If this was what they suffered from, their concept of cure corresponded to the concept of sickness. They wanted to get rid of the symptoms, and their concept of "wellness" was—not to be sick. They wanted to be as well as the average person or, as we also might put it, they wanted to be not more unhappy and disturbed than the average person in our society is.

These people still come to the psychoanalyst to seek help, and for them psychoanalysis is still a therapy which aims at the removal of their symptoms, and at enabling them to function socially. But while they once formed the majority of a psychoanalyst's clientele, they are the minority today—perhaps not because their absolute number is smaller today than then, but because their number is relatively smaller in comparison with the many new "patients" who function socially, who are not sick in the conventional sense, but who do suffer from the "maladie du siècle," the malaise, the inner deadness I have been discussing above. These new "patients" come to the psychoanalyst without knowing what they really suffer from. They complain about being depressed, having insomnia, being unhappy in their marriages, not enjoying their work, and any number of similar troubles. They usually believe that this or that particular symptom is their problem and that if they could get rid of this particular trouble they would be well. However, these patients usually do not see that their problem is not that of depression, of insomnia, of their marriages, or of their jobs. These various complaints are only the conscious form in which our culture permits them to express something which lies much deeper, and which is common to the various people who consciously believe that they suffer from this or that particular symptom. The common suffering is the alienation from oneself, from one's fellow man, and from nature; the awareness that life runs out of one's hand like sand, and that one will die without having lived; that one lives in the midst of plenty and yet is joyless.

What is the help which psychoanalysis can offer those who suffer from the "maladie du siècle"? This help is—and must be—different from the "cure" which consists in removing symptoms, offered to those who cannot function socially. For those who suffer from alienation, cure does not consist in the *absence of illness,* but in the *presence of well-being.*

However, if we are to define well-being, we meet with considerable difficulties. If we stay within the Freudian system, well-being would have to be defined in terms of the libido theory, as the capacity for full genital functioning, or, from a different angle, as the awareness of the hidden Oedipal situation, definitions which, in my opinion, are only tangential to the real problem of human existence and the achievement of well-being by the total man. Any attempt to give a tentative answer to the problem of well-being must transcend the Freudian frame of reference and lead to a discussion, incomplete as it must be, of the basic concept of human existence, which underlies humanistic psychoanalysis. Only in this way can we lay the foundation for the comparison between psychoanalysis and Zen Buddhist thought.

III. THE NATURE OF WELL-BEING—MAN'S PSYCHIC EVOLUTION

The first approach to a definition of well-being can be stated thus: *well-being is being in accord with the nature of man.* If we go beyond this formal statement the question arises: What *is* being, in accordance with the conditions of human existence? What are these conditions?

Human existence poses a question. Man is thrown into this

world without his volition, and taken away from it again without his volition. In contrast to the animal, which in its instincts has a "built-in" mechanism of adaptation to its environment, living completely within nature, man lacks this instinctive mechanism. *He has to live* his life, he *is not lived by* it. He is *in* nature, yet he *transcends* nature; he has awareness of himself, and this awareness of himself as a separate entity makes him feel unbearably alone, lost, powerless. The very fact of being born poses a problem. At the moment of birth, life asks man a question, and this question he must answer. He must answer it at every moment; not his mind, not his body, but *he,* the person who thinks and dreams, who sleeps and eats and cries and laughs—*the whole man*—must answer it. What is this question which life poses? The question is: How can we overcome the suffering, the imprisonment, the shame which the experience of separateness creates; how we can find union within ourselves, with our fellowman, with nature? Man has to answer this question in some way; and even in insanity an answer is given by striking out reality outside of ourselves, living completely within the shell of ourselves, and thus overcoming the fright of separateness.

The *question* is always the same. However, there are *several answers,* or basically, there are only two answers. One is to overcome separateness and to find unity by *regression* to the state of unity which existed before awareness ever arose, that is, before man was born. The other answer is to be *fully born,* to develop one's awareness, one's reason, one's capacity to love, to such a point that one transcends one's own egocentric involvement, and arrives at a new harmony, at a new oneness with the world.

When we speak of birth we usually refer to the act of physiological birth which takes place for the human infant about nine months after conception. But in many ways the significance of this birth is overrated. In important aspects the life of the infant one week after birth is more like intra-uterine existence than like the existence of an adult man or woman. There is, however, a unique aspect of birth: the umbilical cord is severed, and the infant begins his first activity: breathing. Any severance of primary ties, from there on, is possible only to the extent to which this severance is accompanied by genuine activity.

Birth is not one act; it is a process. The aim of life is to be fully born, though its tragedy is that most of us die before we are thus born. To live is to be born every minute. Death occurs when birth stops. Physiologically, our cellular system is in a process of continual birth; psychologically, however, most of us cease to be born at a certain point. Some are completely stillborn; they go on living physiologically when mentally their longing is to return to the womb, to earth, darkness, death; they are insane, or nearly so. Many others proceed further on the path of life. Yet they can not cut the umbilical cord completely, as it were; they remain symbiotically attached to mother, father, family, race, state, status, money, gods, etc.; they never emerge fully as themselves and thus they never become fully born.[8]

The regressive attempt to answer the problem of existence can assume different forms; what is common to all of them is that they necessarily fail and lead to suffering. Once man is

---

[8] The evolution of man from fixation on mother and father, to the point of full independence and enlightenment has been beautifully described by Meister Eckhart in "The Book of Benedictus": "In the first stage the inner or new man, St. Augustine says, follows in the footsteps of good, pious people. He is still an infant at his *mother's* breast.

"In the second stage he no longer follows blindly the example even of good people. He goes in hot pursuit of sound instruction, godly counsel, holy wisdom. He turns his back on man and his face to God: leaving his mother's lap he smiles to his heavenly *Father*.

"In the third stage he parts more and more from his mother, draws further and further away from her breast. He flees care and casts away fear. Though he might with impunity treat everyone with harshness and injustice he would find no satisfaction in it, for in his love to God he is so much engaged with him, so much occupied with him in doing good: God has established him so firmly in joy, in holiness and love that everything unlike and foreign to God seems to him unworthy and repugnant.

"In the fourth state he more and more grows and is rooted in love, in God. He is ever ready to welcome any struggle, any trial, adversity or suffering, and that willingly, gladly, joyfully.

"In the fifth stage he is at peace, enjoying the fullness of supreme ineffable wisdom.

"In the sixth stage he is de-formed and transformed by God's eternal nature. He has come to full perfection and, oblivious of impermanent things and temporal life, is drawn, transported, into the image of God and become a child of God. There is no further and no higher stage. It is eternal rest and bliss. The end of the inner and new man is eternal life." *Meister Eckhart*, translation by C. de B. Evans (London, John M. Watkins, 1952), II, 80-81.

torn away from the prehuman, paradisaical unity with nature, he can never go back to where he came from; two angels with fiery swords block his return. Only in death or in insanity can the return be accomplished—not in life and sanity.

Man can strive to find this regressive unity at several levels, which are at the same time several levels of pathology and irrationality. He can be possessed by the passion to return to the womb, to mother earth, to death. If this aim is all-consuming and unchecked, the result is suicide or insanity. A less dangerous and pathological form of a regressive search for unity is the aim of remaining tied to mother's breast, or to mother's hand, or to father's command. The differences between these various aims mark the differences between various kinds of personalities. The one who remains on mother's breast is the eternally dependent suckling, who has a feeling of euphoria when he is loved, taken care of, protected, and admired, and is filled with unbearable anxiety when threatened with separation from the all-loving mother. The one who remains bound to father's command may develop a good deal of initiative and activity, yet always under the condition that an authority is present who gives orders, who praises and punishes. Another form of regressive orientation lies in destructiveness, in the aim of overcoming separateness by the passion to destroy everything and everybody. One can seek it by the wish to eat up and incorporate everything and everybody, that is, by experiencing the world and everything in it as food, or by outright destruction of everything except the one thing—himself. Still another form of trying to heal the suffering of separateness lies in building up one's own Ego, as a separate, fortified, indestructible "thing." One then experiences oneself as one's own property, one's power, one's prestige, one's intellect.

The individual's emergence from regressive unity is accompanied by the gradual overcoming of narcissism. For the infant shortly after birth there is not even awareness of reality existing outside of himself in the sense of sense-perception; he and mother's nipple and mother's breast are still one; he finds himself in a state *before* any subject-object differentiation takes place. After a while, the capacity for subject-object differentiation develops in every child—but only in the obvious sense of awareness of the difference between me and not-me. But in an *affective* sense, it takes the development of full maturity to overcome the narcissistic attitude of omniscience and omnipotence, provided this stage is ever reached. We observe this narcissistic attitude clearly in the behavior of children and of neurotic persons, except that with the former it is usually conscious, with the latter unconscious. The child does not accept reality as it is, but as he wants it to be. He lives in his wishes, and his view of reality is what he wants it to be. If his wish is not fulfilled, he gets furious, and the function of his fury is to force the world (through the medium of father and mother) to correspond to his wish. In the normal development of the child, this attitude slowly changes to the mature one of being aware of reality and accepting it, its laws, hence necessity. In the neurotic person we find invariably that he has not arrived at this point, and has not given up the narcissistic interpretation of reality. He insists that reality must conform to his ideas, and when he recognizes that this is not so, he reacts either with the impulse to force reality to correspond to his wishes (that is, to do the impossible) or with a feeling of powerlessness because he can not perform the impossible. The notion of freedom which this person has is, whether he is aware of it or not, a notion of narcissistic omnipotence, while the notion of freedom of the fully developed person is that of recognizing reality and its laws and acting within the laws of necessity, by relating oneself to the world productively by grasping the world with one's own powers of thought and affect.

These different goals and the ways to attain them are not primarily different systems of *thought*. They are different *ways of being*, different answers of the total man to the question which life asks him. They are the same answers which have been given in the various religious systems which make up the history of religion. From primitive cannibalism to Zen Buddhism, the human race has given only a few answers to the question of existence, and each man in his own life gives one of these answers, although usually he is not aware of the answer he gives. In our Western culture almost everybody *thinks* that he gives the answer of the Christian or Jewish religions, or the answer of an enlightened atheism, and yet if we could take a mental X ray of everyone, we would find so many adherents of cannibalism, so many of totem worship, so many worshipers of idols of different kinds, and a few Christians, Jews, Buddhists, Taoists. Religion is the formalized and elaborate answer to man's existence, and since it can be shared in consciousness and by ritual with others, even the lowest religion creates a feeling of reasonableness and of security by the very communion with others. When it is not shared, when the regressive wishes are in contrast to consciousness and the claims of the existing culture, then the secret, individual "religion" is a neurosis.

In order to understand the individual patient—or any human being—one must know what *his* answer to the question of existence is, or, to put it differently, what his secret, individual religion is, to which all his efforts and passions are devoted. Most of what one considers to be "psychological problems" are only secondary consequences of his basic "answer," and hence it is rather useless to try to "cure" them before this basic answer—that is, his secret, private religion—has been understood.

Returning now to the question of well-being, how are we going to define it in the light of what has been said thus far?

Well-being is the state of having arrived at the full development of reason: reason not in the sense of a merely intellectual judgment, but in that of grasping truth by "letting things be" (to use Heidegger's term) as they are. Well-being is possible only to the degree to which one has overcome one's narcissism; to the degree to which one is open, responsive, sensitive, awake, empty (in the Zen sense). Well-being means to be fully related to man and nature affectively, to overcome separateness and alienation, to arrive at the experience of oneness with all that exists—and yet to experience *myself* at the same time as the separate entity *I* am, as the in-dividual. Well-being means to be fully born, to become what one potentially is; it means to have the full capacity for joy and for sadness or, to put it still differently, to awake from the half-slumber the average man lives in, and to be fully awake. If it is all that, it means also to be creative; that is, to react and to respond to myself, to others, to everything that exists—to react and to respond as the real, total man I am to the reality of everybody and everything as he or it is. In this act of true response lies the area of creativity, of seeing the world as it is *and* experiencing it as *my* world, the world created and transformed by my creative grasp of it, so that the world ceases to be a strange world "over there" and becomes *my* world. Well-being means, finally, to drop one's Ego, to give up greed, to cease chasing after the preservation and the aggrandizement of the Ego, to be and to experience one's self in the act of being, not in having, preserving, coveting, using.

I have, in the foregoing remarks, tried to point to the parallel development in the individual and in the history of religion. In view of the fact that this paper deals with the relationship of psychonalysis to Zen Buddhism I feel it is necessary to elaborate further on at least some psychological aspects of religious development.

I have said that man is asked a question by the very fact of his existence, and that this is a question raised by the contradiction within himself—that of being in nature and at the same time of transcending nature by the fact that he is life aware of itself. Any man who listens to this question posed to him, and who makes it a matter of "ultimate concern" to answer this question, and to answer it as a whole man and not only by thoughts, is a "religious" man; and all systems that try to give, teach, and transmit such answers are "religions." On the other hand, any man—and any culture—that tries to be deaf to the existential question is irreligious. There is no better example that can be cited for men who are deaf to the question posed by existence than we ourselves, living in the twentieth century. We try to evade the question by concern with property, prestige, power, production, fun, and, ultimately, by trying to forget that we—that I—exist. No matter how often he *thinks* of God or goes to church, or how much he believes in religious ideas, if he, the whole man, is deaf to the question of existence, if he does not have an answer to it, he is marking time, and he lives and dies like one of the million things he produces. He *thinks* of God, instead of experiencing *being* God.

But it is deceptive to think of religions as if they had, necessarily, something in common beyond the concern with giving *an* answer to the question of existence. As far as the *content* of religion is concerned, there is no unity whatsoever; on the contrary, there are two fundamentally opposite answers, which have been mentioned already above with regard to the individual: one answer is to go back to prehuman, preconscious existence, to do away with reason, to become an animal, and thus to become one with nature again. The forms in which this wish is expressed are manifold. At the one pole are phenomena such as we find in the Germanic secret societies of the "berserkers" (literally: "bearshirts") who identified themselves with a bear, in which a young man, during his initiation, had "to transmute his humanity by a fit of aggressive and terror-striking fury, which assimilated him to the raging beast of prey." [9] (That this tendency of returning to the prehuman unity with nature is by no means restricted to primitive societies becomes transparent if we make the connection between the "bearshirts" and Hitler's "brown shirts." While a large sector of the adherents of the National Socialist Party was composed simply of secular, opportunistic, ruthless, power-seeking politicians, Junkers, generals, businessmen, and bureaucrats, the core, represented by the triumvirate of Hitler, Himmler and Goebbels, was essentially not different from the primitive "bearshirts" driven by a "sacred" fury and the aim to destroy as the ultimate fulfillment of their religious vision. These "bearshirts" of the twentieth century who revived the "ritual murder" legend concerning the Jews actually, in doing so, projected one of their own deepest desires: ritual murder. They committed ritual murder first of the Jews, then of foreign populations, then of the German people themselves, and eventually they murdered their own wives and children and themselves in the final rite of complete destruction.) There are many other less archaic religious forms of striving for prehuman unity with nature. They are to be found in cults where the tribe is identified with a totem animal, in religious systems devoted to the worship of trees, lakes, caves, etc., in orgiastic cults which have as their aim the elimination of consciousness, reason, and conscience. In all these religions, the sacred is that which pertains to the vision of man's transmutation into a prehuman part of nature; the "holy man" (for instance, the shaman) is the one who has gone furthest in the achievement of his aim.

The other pole of religion is represented by all those religions which seek the answer to the question of human existence by emerging fully from prehuman existence, by developing the

[9] Mircea Eliade, *Birth and Rebirth* (New York, Harper, 1958), p. 84.

specifically human potentiality of reason and love, and thus by finding a new harmony between man and nature—and between man and man. Although such attempts may be found in individuals of relatively primitive societies, the great dividing line for the whole of humanity seems to lie in the period between roughly 2000 B.C. and the beginning of our era. Taoism and Buddhism in the Far East, Ikhnaton's religious revolutions in Egypt, the Zoroastrian religion in Persia, the Moses religion in Palestine, the Quetzalcoatl religion in Mexico,[10] represent the full turn humanity has taken.

Unity is sought in all these religions—not the regressive unity found by going back to the pre-individual, preconscious harmony of paradise, but unity on a new level: that unity which can be arrived at only after man has experienced his separateness, after he has gone through the stage of alienation from himself and from the world, and has been fully born. This new unity has as a premise the full development of man's reason, leading to a stage in which reason no longer separates man from his immediate, intuitive grasp of reality. There are many symbols for the new goal which lies ahead, and not in the past: Tao, Nirvana, Enlightenment, the Good, God. The differences between these symbols are caused by the social and cultural differences existing in the various countries in which they arose. In the Western tradition the symbol chosen for "the goal" was that of the authoritarian figure of the highest king, or the highest tribal chief. But as early as the time of the Old Testament, this figure changes from that of the arbitrary ruler to that of the ruler bound to man by the covenant and the promises contained therein. In prophetic literature the aim is seen as that of a new harmony between man and nature in the messianic time; in Christianity, God manifests himself as man; in Maimonides' philosophy, as well as in mysticism, the anthropomorphic and authoritarian elements are almost completely eliminated, although in the popular forms of the Western religions they have remained without much change.

What is common to Jewish-Christian and Zen Buddhist thinking is the awareness that I must give up my "will" (in the sense of my desire to force, direct, strangle the world

[10] Cf. Laurette Séjournée's *Burning Waters* (London, Thames & Hudson, 1957).

outside of me and within me) in order to be completely open, responsive, awake, alive. In Zen terminology this is often called "to make oneself empty"—which does not mean something negative, but means the openness to receive. In Christian terminology this is often called "to slay oneself and to accept the will of God." There seems to be little difference between the Christian experience and the Buddhist experience which lies behind the two different formulations. However, as far as the popular interpretation and experience is concerned, this formulation means that instead of making decisions himself, man leaves the decisions to an omniscient, omnipotent father, who watches over him and knows what is good for him. It is clear that in this experience man does not become open and responsive, but obedient and submissive. To follow God's will in the sense of true surrender of egoism is best done if there is no concept of God. Paradoxically, I truly follow God's will if I forget about God. Zen's concept of emptiness implies the true meaning of giving up one's will, yet without the danger of regressing to the idolatrous concept of a helping father.

IV. THE NATURE OF CONSCIOUSNESS, REPRESSION AND DE-REPRESSION

In the foregoing chapter I have tried to outline the ideas of man and of human existence which underlie the goals of humanistic psychoanalysis. But psychoanalysis shares these general ideas with other humanistic philosophical or religious concepts. We must now proceed to describe the specific approach through which psychoanalysis tries to accomplish its goal.

The most characteristic element in the psychoanalytic approach is, without any doubt, its attempt *to make the unconscious conscious*—or, to put it in Freud's words, to transform Id into Ego. But while this formulation sounds simple and clear, it is by no means so. Questions immediately arise: What is the unconscious? What is consciousness? What is repression? How does the unconscious become conscious? And if this happens, what effect does it have?

First of all we must consider that the terms *conscious* and *unconscious* are used with several different meanings. In one meaning, which might be called functional, "conscious" and "unconscious" refer to a subjective state within the individual. Saying that he is conscious of this or that psychic content means that he *is aware* of affects, of desires, of judgments, etc. Unconscious, used in the same sense, refers to a state of mind in which the person is not aware of his inner experiences; if he were totally unaware of *all* experiences, including sensory ones, he would be precisely like a person who *is* unconscious. Saying that the person is conscious of certain affects, etc., means *he is conscious* as far as these affects are concerned; saying that certain affects are unconscious means that he *is* unconscious as far as these contents are concerned. We must remember that "unconscious" does not refer to the absence of any impulse, feeling, desire, fear, etc., but only to the absence of *awareness* of these impulses.

Quite different from the use of conscious and unconscious in the functional sense just described is another use in which one refers to certain localities in the person and to certain contents connected with these localities. This is usually the case if the words "*the* conscious" and "*the* unconscious" are used. Here "the conscious" is *one part of the personality,* with specific contents, and "the unconscious" is another part of the personality, with other specific contents. In Freud's view, the unconscious is essentially the seat of irrationality. In Jung's thinking, the meaning seems to be almost reversed; the unconscious is essentially the seat of the deepest sources of wisdom, while the conscious is the intellectual part of the personality. In this view of the conscious and the unconscious, the latter is perceived as being like the cellar of a house, in which everything is piled up that has no place in the superstructure; Freud's cellar contains mainly man's vices; Jung's contains mainly man's wisdom.

As H. S. Sullivan has emphasized, the use of "the unconscious" in the sense of locality is unfortunate, and a poor representation of the psychic facts involved. I might add that the preference for this kind of substantive rather than for functional concept corresponds to the general tendency in contemporary Western culture to perceive in terms of things we *have,* rather than to perceive in terms of *being.* We *have* a problem of anxiety, we *have* insomnia, we *have* a depression, we *have* a psychoanalyst, just as we have a car, a house, or a child. In the same vein we also *have* an "unconscious." It is not accidental that many people use the word "subconscious" instead of the word "unconscious." They do it obviously for the reason that "subconscious" lends itself better to the localized concept; I can say "I am unconscious of" this or that, but I cannot say "I am subconscious" of it.

There exists still another use of "conscious," which sometimes leads to confusion. Consciousness is identified with *reflecting intellect,* the unconscious with unreflected experience. There can, of course, be no objection to this use of conscious and unconscious, provided the meaning is clear and not confused with the other two meanings. Nevertheless, this use does not seem fortunate; intellectual reflection is, of course, always conscious, but not all that is conscious is intellectual reflection. If I look at a person, I am *aware* of the person, I am aware of whatever happens in me in relation to the person, but only if I have separated myself from him in a subject-object distance is this consciousness identical with intellectual reflection. The same holds true if I am aware of my breathing, which is by no means the same as *thinking about* my breathing; in fact, once I begin to think *about* my breathing, I am not aware of my breathing any more. The same holds true for all my acts of relating myself to the world. More will be said about this later on.

Having decided to speak of unconscious and conscious as states of awareness and unawareness, respectively, rather than as "parts" of personality and specific contents, we must now consider the question of what prevents an experience from reaching our awareness—that is, from becoming conscious.

But before we begin to discuss this question, another one arises which should be answered first. If we speak in a psychoanalytic context of consciousness and unconsciousness, there is an implication that consciousness is of a higher value than unconsciousness. Why should we be striving to broaden the domain of consciousness, unless this were so? Yet it is quite obvious that consciousness as such has no particular value; in fact, most of what people have in their conscious minds is fiction and delusion; this is the case not so much because people would be *incapable* of seeing the truth as because of the function of society. Most of human history (with the exception of some primitive societies) is characterized by the fact that a small minority has ruled over and exploited the majority of its fellows. In order to do so, the minority has usually used force; but force is not enough. In the long run, the majority has had to accept its own exploitation voluntarily—and this is only possible if its mind has been filled with all sorts of lies and fictions, justifying and explaining its acceptance of the minority's rule. However, this is not the only reason for the fact that most of what people have in their awareness about themselves, others, society, etc., is fiction. In its historical development each society becomes caught in its own need to survive in the particular form in which it has developed, and it usually accomplishes this survival by ignoring the wider human aims which are common to all men. This contradiction between the social and the universal aim leads also to the fabrication (on a social scale) of all sorts of fictions and illusions which have the function to deny and to rationalize the dichotomy between the goals of humanity and those of a given society.

We might say, then, that the content of consciousness is mostly fictional and delusional, and precisely does not represent reality. Consciousness as such, then, is nothing desirable. Only if the hidden reality (that which is unconscious) is revealed, and hence is no longer hidden (i.e., has become conscious)—has something valuable been achieved. We shall come back to this discussion at a later point. Right now I want only to emphasize that most of what is in our consciousness is "false consciousness" and that it is essentially society that fills us with these fictitious and unreal notions.

But the effect of society is not only to funnel fictions into our consciousness, also to prevent the awareness of reality. The further elaboration of this point leads us straight into the central problem of how repression or unconsciousness occurs.

The animal has a consciousness of the things around it which, to use R. M. Bucke's term, we may call "simple consciousness." Man's brain structure, being larger and more complex than that of the animal transcends this simple consciousness and is the basis of *self consciousness*, awareness of himself as the subject of his experience. But perhaps because of its enormous complexity [11] human awareness is organized in various possible ways, and for any experience to come into awareness, it must be comprehensible in the categories in which conscious thought is organized. Some of the categories, such as time and space, may be universal, and may constitute categories of perception common to all men. Others, such as causality, may be a valid category for many, but not for all, forms of human conscious perception. Other categories are even less general and differ from culture to culture. However this may be, experience can enter into awareness only under the condition that it can be perceived, related, and ordered in terms of a conceptual system [12] and of its categories. This system is in itself a result of social evolution. Every society, by its own practice of living and by the mode of relatedness, of feeling, and perceiving, develops a system of categories which determines the forms of awareness. This system works, as it were, like a *socially conditioned filter;* experience cannot enter awareness unless it can penetrate this filter.

The question then, is to understand more concretely how this "social filter" operates, and how it happens that it permits certain experiences to be filtered through, while others are stopped from entering awareness.

First of all, we must consider that many experiences do not lend themselves easily to being perceived in awareness. Pain is perhaps the physical experience which best lends itself to being consciously perceived; sexual desire, hunger, etc., also are easily perceived; quite obviously, all sensations which are relevant to individual or group survival have easy access to

[11] I have been greatly stimulated in my thinking by personal communications from Dr. William Wolf on the neurological basis of consciousness.

[12] The same idea has been expressed by E. Schachtel (in an illuminating paper on "Memory and Childhood Amnesia," in *Psychiatry,* Vol. X, no. 1, 1947) with regard to the amnesia of childhood memories. As the title indicates, he is concerned there with the more specific problem of childhood amnesia, and with the difference between the categories ("schematas") employed by the child and those employed by the adult. He concludes that "the incompatibility of early childhood experience with the categories and organization of adult memory is to a large extent due to . . . the conventionalization of the adult memory." In my opinion, what he says about childhood and adult memory holds true, but we find not only the differences between childhood and adult categories, but also those between various cultures, and furthermore, the problem is not only that of memory, but also that of consciousness in general.

awareness. But when it comes to a more subtle or complex experience, like *seeing a rosebud in the early morning, a drop of dew on it, while the air is still chilly, the sun coming up, a bird singing*—this is an experience which in some cultures easily lends itself to awareness (for instance, in Japan), while in modern Western culture this same experience will usually not come into awareness because it is not sufficiently "important" or "eventful" to be noticed. Whether or not subtle affective experiences can arrive at awareness depends on the degree to which such experiences are cultivated in a given culture. There are many affective experiences for which a given language has no word, while another language may be rich in words which express these feelings. In English, for instance, we have one word, "love," which covers experiences ranging from liking to erotic passion to brotherly and motherly love. In a language in which different affective experiences are not expressed by different words, it is almost impossible for one's experiences to come to awareness, and vice versa. Generally speaking, it may be said that an experience rarely comes into awareness for which the language has no word.

But this is only one aspect of the filtering function of language. Different languages differ not only by the fact that they vary in the diversity of words they use to denote certain affective experiences, but by their syntax, their grammar, and the root-meaning of their words. The whole language contains an attitude of life, is a frozen expression of experiencing life in a certain way.[13]

Here are a few examples. There are languages in which the verb form "it rains," for instance, is conjugated differently depending on whether I say that it rains because I have been out in the rain and have got wet, or because I have seen it raining from the inside of a hut, or because somebody has told me that it rains. It is quite obvious that the emphasis of the language on these different *sources* of experiencing a fact (in this case, that it rains) has a deep influence on *the way* people experience facts. (In our modern culture, for instance, with its emphasis on the purely intellectual side of knowledge, it makes little difference how I know a fact, whether from direct

[13] Cf. the pathfinding contribution of Benjamin Whorf in his *Collected Papers on Metalinguistics* (Washington, D.C., Foreign Service Institute, 1952).

or indirect experience, or from hearsay.) Or, in Hebrew the main principle of conjugation is to determine whether an activity is complete (perfect) or incomplete (imperfect), while the time in which it occurs—past, present, future—is expressed only in a secondary fashion. In Latin both principles (time and perfection) are used together, while in English we are predominantly oriented in the sense of time. Again, it goes without saying that this difference in conjugation expresses a difference in experiencing.[14]

Still another example is to be found in the different use of verbs and nouns in various languages, or even among different people speaking the same language. The noun refers to a "thing"; the verb refers to an activity. An increasing number of people prefer to think in terms of *having things,* instead of *being* or *acting;* hence they prefer nouns to verbs.

Language, by its words, its grammar, its syntax, by the whole spirit which is frozen in it, determines how we experience, and which experiences penetrate to our awareness.

The second aspect of the filter which makes awareness possible is the *logic* which directs the thinking of people in a given culture. Just as most people assume that their language is "natural" and that other languages only use different words for the same things, they assume also that the rules which determine proper thinking, are natural and universal ones; that what is illogical in one cultural system is illogical in any other, because it conflicts with "natural" logic. A good example of this is the difference between Aristotelian and paradoxical logic.

Aristotelian logic is based on the law of identity which states that A is A, the law of contradiction (A is not non-A), and the law of the excluded middle (A cannot be A *and* non-A, neither A *nor* non-A). Aristotle stated it: "It is impossible for the same thing at the same time to belong and not to belong to the same thing and in the same respect. . . . This, then, is the most certain of all principles." [15]

In opposition to Aristotelian logic is what one might call

<hr />

[14] The significance of this difference becomes quite apparent in the English and German translations of the Old Testament; often when the Hebrew text uses the perfect tense for an emotional experience like loving, meaning, "I love fully," the translator misunderstands and writes "I loved."

[15] Aristotle, Metaphysics, Book Gamma, 1005b 20. Quoted from Aristotle's Metaphysics, transl. by R. Hope (Columbia Univ. Press, New York, 1952).

paradoxical logic, which assumes that A and non-A do not exclude each other as predicates of X. Paradoxical logic was predominant in Chinese and Indian thinking, in Heraclitus' philosophy, and then again under the name of dialectics in the thought of Hegel and Marx. The general principle of paradoxical logic has been clearly described in general terms by Lao-Tse: "Words that are strictly true seem to be paradoxical." [16] And by Chuang-tzu: "That which is one is one. That which is not-one, is also one."

Inasmuch as a person lives in a culture in which the correctness of Aristotelian logic is not doubted, it is exceedingly difficult, if not impossible, for him to be aware of experiences which contradict Aristotelian logic, hence which from the standpoint of his culture are nonsensical. A good example is Freud's concept of ambivalence, which says that one can experience love and hate for the same person at the same time. This experience, which from the standpoint of paradoxical logic is quite "logical," does not make sense from the standpoint of Aristotelian logic. As a result, it is exceedingly difficult for most people to be aware of feelings of ambivalence. If they are aware of love, they can not be aware of hate—since it would be utterly non-sensical to have two contradictory feelings at the same time towards the same person.[17]

The third aspect of the filter, aside from language and logic, is the *content* of experiences. Every society excludes certain thoughts and feelings from being thought, felt, and expressed. There are things which are not only "not done" but which are even "not thought." In a tribe of warriors, for instance, whose members live by killing and robbing members of other tribes, there might be an individual who feels revulsion against killing and robbing. Yet it is most unlikely that he will be aware of this feeling, since it would be incompatible with the feeling of the whole tribe; to be aware of this incompatible feeling would mean the danger of feeling completely isolated and ostracized. Hence an individual with such a feeling of revulsion would probably develop a psychoso-

[16] Lao-Tse, "The Tâo Teh King," "The Sacred Books of the East," ed. by F. Max Mueller, Vol. XXXIX (Oxford University Press, London, 1927, p. 120).
[17] Cf. my more detailed discussion of this problem in *The Art of Loving,* World Perspectives Series (Harper & Bros., New York, 1956, p. 72 ff).

matic symptom of vomiting, instead of letting the feeling of revulsion penetrate to his awareness.

Exactly the contrary would be found in a member of a peaceful agricultural tribe, who has the impulse to go out and kill and rob members of other groups. He also would probably not permit himself to become aware of his impulses, but instead, would develop a symptom—maybe intense fright. Still another example: There must be many shopkeepers in our big cities who have a customer who badly needs, let us say, a suit of clothes, but who does not have sufficient money to buy even the cheapest one. Among those shopkeepers there must be a few who have the natural human impulse to give the suit to the customer for the price that he can pay. But how many of these shopkeepers will permit themselves to be aware of such an impulse? I assume very few. The majority will repress it, and we might find among these men some aggressive behavior toward the customer which hides the unconscious impulse, or a dream the following night which expresses it.

In stating the thesis that contents which are incompatible with socially permissible ones are not permitted to enter the realm of awareness, we raise two further questions. Why are certain contents incompatible with a given society? Furthermore, why is the individual so afraid of being aware of such forbidden contents?

As to the first question, I must refer to the concept of the "social character." Any society, in order to survive, must mold the character of its members in such a way that *they want to do what they have to do;* their social function must become internalized and transformed into something they feel driven to do, rather than something they are obliged to do. A society cannot permit deviation from this pattern, because if this "social character" loses its coherence and firmness, many individuals would cease to act as they are expected to do, and the survival of the society in its given form would be endangered. Societies, of course, differ in the rigidity with which they enforce their social character, and the observation of the taboos for protecting this character, but in all societies there are taboos, the violation of which results in ostracism.

The second question is why the individual is so afraid of the implied danger of ostracism that he does not permit himself to be aware of the "forbidden" impulses. To answer this question, I must also refer to fuller statements made elsewhere.[18] To put it briefly, unless he is to become insane, he has to relate himself in some way to others. To be completely unrelated brings him to the frontier of insanity. While in so far as he is an animal he is most afraid of dying, in so far as he is a man he is most afraid of being utterly alone. This fear, rather than, as Freud assumes, castration fear, is the effective agent which does not permit awareness of tabooed feelings and thoughts.

We come, then, to the conclusion that consciousness and unconsciousness are socially conditioned. *I am aware* of all my feelings and thoughts which are permitted to penetrate the threefold filter of (socially conditioned) language, logic, and taboos (social character). Experiences which can not be filtered through remain outside of awareness; that is, they remain unconscious.[19]

Two qualifications have to be made in connection with the emphasis on the social nature of the unconscious. One, a rather obvious one, is that in addition to the social taboos there are individual elaborations of these taboos which differ from family to family; a child, afraid of being "abandoned" by his parents because he is aware of experiences which to them individually are taboo, will, in addition to the socially normal repression, also repress those feelings which are prevented from coming to awareness by the individual aspect of the filter. On the other hand, parents with great inner openness and with little "repressedness" will, by their own influence, tend to make the social filter (and Superego) less narrow and impenetrable.

The other qualification refers to a more complicated phenomenon. We repress not only the awareness of those strivings which are incompatible with the social pattern of thought, we tend also to repress those strivings which are incompatible with the principle of structure and growth of the whole human being, incompatible with the "humanistic conscience," that

---

[18] Cf. my descriptions of this concept in *Escape from Freedom* (New York, Rinehart, 1941) and *The Sane Society* (New York, Rinehart, 1955).

[19] Thi⸱ ⸱ of consciousness leads to the same conclusion Karl Marx reached when ne formulated the problem of consciousness: "It is not the consciousness of men that determines their existence but, on the contrary, it is their social existence that determines their consciousness" (*Zur Kritik u. r Politischen Oekonomie* [Berlin, Dietz, 1924], foreword, p. LV).

voice which speaks in the name of the full development of our person.

Destructive impulses, or the impulse to regress to the womb, or to death, the impulse to eat up those whom I want to be close to—all those and many other regressive impulses may or may not be compatible with the social character, but they are under no circumstances compatible with the inherent goals of the evolution of man's nature. When an infant wants to be nursed it is normal, that is, it corresponds to the state of evolution in which the infant is at the time. If an adult has the same aims, he is ill; inasmuch as he is not only prompted by the past, but also by the goal which is inherent in his total structure, he senses the discrepancy between what he is and what he ought to be; "ought" being used here not in the moral sense of a command, but in the sense of the immanent evolutionary goals inherent in the chromosomes from which he develops, just as his future physical build, the color of his eyes, etc., are already "present" in the chromosomes.

If man loses his contact with the social group he lives in, he becomes afraid of utter isolation, and because of this fear he does not dare to think what "is not thought." But man is also afraid of being completely isolated from humanity, which is inside of him and represented by his conscience. To be completely inhuman is frightening too, although as historical evidence seems to indicate, less frightening than to be socially ostracized, provided a whole society has adopted inhuman norms of behavior. The more a society approximates the human norm of living, the less is there a conflict between isolation from society and from humanity. The greater the conflict between social aims and human aims, the more is the individual torn between the two dangerous poles of isolation. It hardly needs to be added that to the degree to which a person—by his own intellectual and spiritual development—feels his solidarity with humanity, the more can he tolerate social ostracism, and vice versa. The ability to act according to one's conscience depends on the degree to which one has transcended the limits of one's society and has become a citizen of the world, a "cosmopolitan."

The individual cannot permit himself to be aware of thoughts or feelings which are incompatible with the patterns of his culture, and hence he is forced to repress them. *Formally* speaking, then, what is unconscious and what is conscious depends (aside from the individual, family-conditioned elements and the influence of humanistic conscience) on the structure of society and on the patterns of feelings and thoughts it produces. As to the *contents of the unconscious,* no generalization is possible. But one statement can be made: it always represents the whole man, with all his potentialities for darkness and light; it always contains the basis for the different answers which man is capable of giving to the question which existence poses. In the extreme case of the most regressive cultures, bent on returning to animal existence, this very wish is predominant and conscious, while all striving to emerge from this level are repressed. In a culture which has moved from the regressive to the spiritual-progressive goal, the forces representing the dark are unconscious. But man, in any culture, has all the potentialities; he is the archaic man, the beast of prey, the cannibal, the idolater, and he is the being with the capacity for reason, for love, for justice. The content of the unconscious, then, is neither the good nor the evil, the rational nor the irrational; it is both; it is all that is human. The unconscious is the whole man—minus that part of man which corresponds to his society. Consciousness represents social man, the accidental limitations set by the historical situation into which an individual is thrown. Unconsciousness represents universal man, the whole man, rooted in the Cosmos; it represents the plant in him, the animal in him, the spirit in him; it represents his past down to the dawn of human existence, and it represents his future to the day when man will have become fully human, and when nature will be humanized as man will be "naturalized."

Defining consciousness and unconsciousness as we have done, what does it mean if we speak of *making the unconscious conscious, of de-repression?*

In Freud's concept, making the unconscious conscious had a limited function, first of all because the unconscious was supposed to consist mainly of the repressed, instinctual desires, as far as they are incompatible with civilized life. He dealt with single instinctual desires such as incestuous impulses, castration fear, penis envy, etc., the awareness of which was assumed to have been repressed in the history of a particular individual. The awareness of the repressed impulse was supposed to be conducive to its domination by the victorious ego. When we free ourselves from the limited concept of Freud's unconscious and follow the concept presented above, then Freud's aim, the transformation of unconsciousness into consciousness ("Id into Ego"), gains a wider and more profound meaning. *Making the unconscious conscious transforms the mere idea of the universality of man into the living experience of this universality; it is the experiential realization of humanism.*

Freud saw clearly how repression interferes with a person's sense of reality, and how the lifting of repression leads to a new appreciation of reality. Freud called the distorting effect of unconscious strivings "transference"; H. S. Sullivan later on called the same phenomenon "parataxic distortion." Freud discovered, first in the relationship of the patient to the analyst, that the patient did not see the analyst *as he is,* but as a projection of his (the patient's) own expectations, desires, and anxieties as they were originally formed in his experiences with the significant persons of his childhood. Only when the patient gets in touch with his unconscious can he overcome the distortions produced by himself and see the person of the analyst, as well as that of his father or his mother, as it is.

What Freud discovered here was the fact that we see reality in a distorted way. That we believe to see a person as he is, while actually we see our projection of an image of the person without being aware of it. Freud saw not only the distorting influence of transference, but also the many other distorting influences of repression. Inasmuch as a person is motivated by impulses unknown to him, and in contrast to his conscious thinking (representing the demands of social reality), he may project his own unconscious strivings unto another person, and hence not be aware of them within himself but—with indignation—in the other ("projection"). Or, he may invent rational reasons for impulses which in themselves have an entirely different source. This conscious reasoning, which is a pseudo-explanation for aims the true motives of which are unconscious, Freud called *rationalizations.* Whether we deal with transference, projection, or with rationalizations, most of what the person is conscious of is a fiction—while that which he represses (i.e., which is unconscious) is real.

Taking into account what has been said above about the stultifying influence of society, and furthermore considering our wider concept of what constitutes unconsciousness, we arrive at a new concept of unconsciousness—consciousness. We may begin by saying that the average person, while he thinks he is awake, actually is half asleep. By "half asleep" I mean that his contact with reality is a very partial one; most of what he believes to be reality (outside or inside of himself) is a set of fictions which his mind constructs. He is aware of reality only to the degree to which his social functioning make it necessary. He is aware of his fellowmen inasmuch as he needs to cooperate with them; he is aware of material and social reality inasmuch as he needs to be aware of it in order to manipulate it. *He is aware of reality to the extent to which the goal of survival makes such awareness necessary.* (In contradistinction in the state of sleep the awareness of outer reality is suspended, though easily recovered in case of necessity, and in the case of insanity, full awareness of outer reality is absent and not even recoverable in any kind of emergency.) The average person's consciousness is mainly "false consciousness," consisting of fictions and illusion, while precisely what he is not aware of is reality. We can thus differentiate between what a person *is* conscious of, and what he *becomes* conscious of. He *is* conscious, mostly, of fictions; he can *become* conscious of the realities which lie underneath these fictions.

There is another aspect of unconsciousness which follows from the premises discussed earlier. Inasmuch as consciousness represents only the small sector of socially patterned experience and unconsciousness represents the richness and depth of universal man the state of repressedness results in the fact that I, the accidental, social person, am separated from me the whole human person. I am a stranger to myself, and to the same degree everybody else is a stranger to me. I am cut off from the vast area of experience which is human, and remain a fragment of a man, a cripple who experiences only a small part of what is real in him and what is real in others.

Thus far we have spoken only of the distorting function of repressedness; another aspect remains to be mentioned which does not lead to distortion, but to making an experience unreal by *cerebration*. I refer by this to the fact that I believe I see— but I only *see words;* I believe I feel, but I only *think feelings*. The cerebrating person is the alienated person, the person in the cave who, as in Plato's allegory, sees only shadows and mistakes them for immediate reality.

This process of cerebration is related to the ambiguity of language. As soon as I have expressed something in a word, an alienation takes place, and the full experience has already been substituted for by the word. The full experience actually exists only up to the moment when it is expressed in language. This general process of cerebration is more widespread and intense in modern culture than it probably was at any time before in history. Just because of the increasing emphasis on intellectual knowledge which is a condition for scientific and technical achievements, and in connection with it on literacy and education, words more and more take the place of experience. Yet the person concerned is unaware of this. He thinks he sees something; he thinks he feels something; yet there is no experience except memory and thought. When he thinks *he* grasps reality it is only his brain-self that grasps it, while he, the whole man, his eyes, his hands, his heart, his belly, grasp nothing—in fact, *he* is not participating in the experience which he believes is *his*.

What happens then in the process in which the unconscious becomes conscious? In answering this question we had better reformulate it. There is no such thing as "the conscious" and no such thing as "the unconscious." There are degrees of consciousness-awareness and unconsciousness-unawareness. Our question then should rather be: what happens when I become aware of what I have not been aware of before? In line with what has been said before, the general answer to this question is that every step in this process is in the direction of understanding the fictitious, unreal character of our "normal" consciousness. To become conscious of what is unconscious and thus to enlarge one's consciousness means to get in touch with reality, and—in this sense—with truth (intellectually and affectively). To enlarge consciousness means to wake up, to lift a veil, to leave the cave, to bring light into the darkness.

Could this be the same experience Zen Buddhists call "enlightenment"?

While I shall return later to this question, I want at this point to discuss further a crucial point for psychoanalysis, namely, the *nature of insight and knowledge* which is to affect the transformation of unconsciousness into consciousness.[20] Doubtlessly, in the first years of his psychoanalytic research Freud shared the conventional rationalistic belief that knowledge was intellectual, theoretical knowledge. He thought that it was enough to explain to the patient why certain developments had taken place, and to tell him what the analyst discovered in his unconscious. This intellectual knowledge, called "interpretation," was supposed to effect a change in the patient. But soon Freud and other analysts had to discover the truth of Spinoza's statement that *intellectual* knowledge is conducive to change only inasmuch as it is also *affective* knowledge. It became apparent that intellectual knowledge as such does not produce any change, except perhaps in the sense that by intellectual knowledge of his unconscious strivings a person may be better able to control them—which, however, is the aim of traditional ethics, rather than that of psychoanalysis. As long as the patient remains in the attitude of the detached scientific observer, taking himself as the object of his investigation, he is not in touch with his unconscious, except by *thinking* about it; he does not *experience* the wider, deeper reality within himself. Discovering one's unconscious is, precisely, *not* an intellectual act, but an affective experience, which can hardly be put into words, if at all. This does not mean that thinking and speculation may not precede the act of discovery; but the act of discovery itself is always a *total* experience. It is total in the sense that the whole person experiences it; it is an experience which is characterized by its spontaneity and suddenness. One's eyes are suddenly opened; oneself and the world appear in a different light, are seen from a different viewpoint. There is usually a good deal of anxiety aroused before the experience takes place, while afterwards a new feeling of strength and certainty is present. The process of discovering the unconscious

---

[20] We have no word to express this transformation. We could say "reversion of repressedness," or, more concretely, "awakening"; I propose the term "de-repression."

can be described as a series of ever-widening experiences, which are felt deeply and which transcend theoretical, intellectual knowledge.

The importance of this kind of *experiential knowledge* lies in the fact that it transcends the kind of knowledge and awareness in which the subject-intellect observes himself as an object, and thus that it transcends the Western, rationalistic concept of knowing. (Exceptions in the Western tradition, where experiential knowledge is dealt with, are to be found in Spinoza's highest form of knowing, intuition; in Fichte's intellectual intuition; or in Bergson's creative consciousness. All these categories of intuition transcend subject-object split knowledge. The importance of this kind of experience for the problem of Zen Buddhism will be clarified later, in the discussion of Zen.)

One more point in our brief sketch of the essential elements in psychoanalysis needs to be mentioned, *the role of the psychoanalyst.* Originally it was not different from that of any physician "treating" a patient. But after some years the situation changed radically. Freud recognized that the analyst himself needed to be analyzed, that is, to undergo the same process his patient was to submit to later. This need for the analyst's analysis was explained as resulting from the necessity to free the analyst from his own blind spots, neurotic tendencies, and so on. But this explanation seems insufficient, as far as Freud's own views are concerned, if we consider Freud's early statements, quoted above, when he spoke of the analyst needing to be a "model," a "teacher," being able to conduct a relationship between himself and the patient which is based on a "love of truth," that precludes any kind of "sham or deception." Freud seems to have sensed here that the analyst has a function transcending that of the physician in his relationship to his patient. But still, he did not change his fundamental concept, that of the analyst being the detached observer—and the patient being his *object* of observation. In the history of psychoanalysis, this concept of the detached observer was modified from two sides, first by Ferenczi, who in the last years of his life postulated that it was not enough for the analyst to observe and to interpret; that he had to be able to love the patient with the very love which the patient had needed as a child, yet had never experienced. Ferenczi did not have in mind that the analyst should feel erotic love toward his patient, but rather motherly or fatherly love or, putting it more generally, loving care.[21] H. S. Sullivan approached the same point from a different aspect. He thought that the analyst must not have the attitude of a detached observer, but of a *"participant observer,"* thus trying to transcend the orthodox idea of the detachment of the analyst. In my own view, Sullivan may not have gone far enough, and one might prefer the definition of the analyst's role as that of an *"observant participant,"* rather than that of a participant observer. But even the expression "participant" does not quite express what is meant here; to "participate" is still to be outside. The knowledge of another person requires being inside of him, to *be* him. The analyst understands the patient only inasmuch as he experiences in himself all that the patient experiences; otherwise he will have only intellectual knowledge *about* the patient, but will never really know what the patient experiences, nor will he be able to convey to him that he shares and understands his (the patient's) experience. In this productive relatedness between analyst and patient, in the act of being fully engaged with the patient, in being fully open and responsive to him, in being soaked with him, as it were, in this center-to-center relatedness, lies one of the essential conditions for psychoanalytic understanding and cure.[22] The analyst must become the patient, yet he must be himself; he must forget that he is the doctor, yet he must remain aware of it. Only when he accepts this paradox, can he give "interpretations" which carry authority because they are rooted in his own experience. The analyst analyzes the patient, but the patient also analyzes the analyst, because the analyst, by sharing the unconscious of his patient, cannot help clarifying his own unconscious. Hence the analyst not only cures the patient, but is also cured by him. He not only understands the patient, but eventually the patient understands him. When this stage is reached, solidarity and communion are reached.

This relationship to the patient must be realistic and free

21 Cf. S. Ferenczi, *Collected Papers,* ed. by Clara Thompson (Basic Books, Inc.), and the excellent study of Ferenczi's ideas in Izette de Forest's *The Leaven of Love* (New York, Harper, 1954).

22 Cf. my paper on "The Limitations and Dangers of Psychology," published in *Religion and Culture,* ed. by W. Leibrecht (New York, Harper, 1959).

from all sentimentality. Neither the analyst nor any man can "save" another human being. He can act as a guide—or as a midwife; he can show the road, remove obstacles, and sometimes lend some direct help, but he can never do for the patient what only the patient can do for himself. He must make this perfectly clear to the patient, not only in words, but by his whole attitude. He must also stress the awareness of the realistic situation which is even more limited than a relationship between two persons necessarily needs to be; if he, the analyst, is to live his own life, and if he is to serve a number of patients simultaneously, there are limitations in time and space. But there is no limitation in the here and now of the encounter between patient and analyst. When this encounter takes place, during the analytic session, when the two talk to each other, then there is nothing more important in the world than their talking to each other—for the patient as well as for the analyst. The analyst, in years of common work with the patient, transcends indeed the conventional role of the doctor; he becomes a teacher, a model, perhaps a master, provided that he himself never considers himself as analyzed until he has attained full self-awareness and freedom, until he has overcome his own alienation and separateness. The didactic analysis of the analyst is not the end, but the beginning of a continuous process of self analysis, that is, of ever-increasing awakeness.

V. PRINCIPLES OF ZEN BUDDHISM

In the foregoing pages I have given a brief sketch of Freudian psychoanalysis and its continuation in humanistic psychoanalysis. I have discussed man's existence and the question it poses; the nature of well-being defined as the overcoming of alienation and separateness; the specific method by which psychoanalysis tries to attain its goal, namely, the penetration of the unconscious. I have dealt with the question of what the nature of unconsciousness and of consciousness is; and what "knowing" and "awareness" mean in psychoanalysis; finally, I have discussed the role of the analyst in the process.

In order to prepare the ground for a discussion of the relationship between psychoanalysis and Zen, it seems as though I should have to give a systematic picture of Zen Buddhism.

Fortunately, there is no need for such an attempt, since Dr. Suzuki's lectures in this book (as well as his other writings) have precisely the aim of transmitting an understanding of the nature of Zen as far as it can be given at all in words. However, I must speak of those principles of Zen which have an immediate bearing on psychoanalysis.

The essence of Zen is the acquisition of enlightenment *(satori)*. One who has not had this experience can never fully understand Zen. Since I have not experienced *satori,* I can talk about Zen only in a tangential way, and not as it ought to be talked about—out of the fullness of experience. But this is not, as C. G. Jung has suggested, because *satori* "depicts an art and a way of enlightenment which is practically impossible for the European to appreciate." [23] As far as this goes, Zen is not more difficult for the European than Heraclitus, Meister Eckhart, or Heidegger. The difficulty lies in the tremendous effort which is required to acquire *satori;* this effort is more than most people are willing to undertake, and that is why *satori* is rare even in Japan. Nevertheless, even though I cannot talk of Zen with any authority, the good fortune of having read Dr. Suzuki's books, heard quite a few of his lectures, and read whatever else was available to me on Zen Buddhism, has given me at least an approximate idea of what constitutes Zen, an idea which I hope enables me to make a tentative comparison between Zen Buddhism and psychoanalysis.

What is the basic aim of Zen? To put it in Suzuki's words: "Zen in its essence is the art of seeing into the nature of one's being, and it points the way from bondage to freedom. . . . We can say that Zen liberates all the energies properly and naturally stored in each of us, which are in ordinary circumstances cramped and distorted so that they find no adequate channel for activity. . . . It is the object of Zen, therefore, to save us from going crazy or being crippled. This is what I mean by freedom, giving free play to all the creative and benevolent impulses inherently lying in our hearts. Generally, we are blind to this fact, that we are in possession of all the necessary faculties that will make us happy and loving towards

[23] Foreword to D. T. Suzuki, *Introduction to Zen Buddhism* (London, Rider, 1949), pp. 9-10.

one another." [24] We find in this definition a number of essential aspects of Zen which I should like to emphasize: Zen is the art of *seeing into the nature of one's being;* it is a way *from bondage to freedom;* it *liberates our natural energies;* it *prevents us from going crazy or being crippled;* and it impels us to express our faculty for *happiness and love.*

The final aim of Zen is the experience of enlightenment, called *satori.* Dr. Suzuki has given, in these lectures, and in his other writings, as much of a description as can be given at all. In these remarks I would like to stress some aspects which are of special importance for the Western reader, and especially for the psychologist. *Satori* is *not* an abnormal state of mind; it is *not* a trance in which reality disappears. It is not a narcissistic state of mind, as it can be seen in some religious manifestations. "If anything, it is a perfectly normal state of mind. . . ." As Jōshū declared, "Zen is your everyday thought," it all depends on the adjustment of the hinge, whether the door opens in or opens out." [25] *Satori* has a peculiar effect on the person who experiences it. "All your mental activities will now be working in a different key, which will be more satisfying, more peaceful, more full of joy than anything you ever experienced before. The tone of life will be altered. There is something rejuvenating in the possession of Zen. The spring flower will look prettier, and the mountain stream runs cooler and more transparent." [26]

It is quite clear that *satori* is the true fulfillment of the state of well-being which Dr. Suzuki described in the passage quoted above. If we would try to express enlightenment in psychological terms, I would say that it is a state in which the person is completely tuned to the reality outside and inside of him, a state in which he is fully aware of it and fully grasps it. *He* is aware of it—that is, not his brain, nor any other part of his organism, but *he,* the whole man. He is aware of *it;* not as of an object over there which he grasps with his thought, but *it,* the flower, the dog, the man, in its, or his, full reality. He who awakes is open and responsive to the world, and he can be open

[24] D. T. Suzuki, *Zen Buddhism* (New York, Doubleday Anchor Book, 1956), p. 3.
[25] D. T. Suzuki, *Introduction to Zen Buddhism* (London, Rider, 1949), p. 97.
[26] *Ibid.,* pp. 97-98.

and responsive because he has given up holding on to himself as a thing, and thus has become empty and ready to receive. To be enlightened means "the full awakening of the total personality to reality."

It is very important to understand that the state of enlightenment is not a state of dissociation or of a trance in which one *believes* oneself to be awakened, when one is actually deeply asleep. The Western psychologist, of course, will be prone to believe that *satori* is just a subjective state, an auto-induced sort of trance, and even a psychologist as sympathetic to Zen as Dr. Jung cannot avoid the same error. Jung writes: "The imagination itself is a psychic occurrence, and therefore, whether an enlightenment is called real or imaginary is quite immaterial. The man who has enlightenment, or alleges that he has it, thinks in any case that he is enlightened. . . . Even if he were to lie, his lie would be a spiritual fact." [27] This is, of course, part of Jung's general relativistic position with regard to the "truth" of religious experience. Contrary to him, I believe that a lie is never "a spiritual fact," nor any other fact, for that matter, except that of being a lie. But whatever the merits of the case, Jung's position is certainly not shared by Zen Buddhists. On the contrary, it is of crucial importance for them to differentiate between genuine *satori* experience, in which the acquisition of a new viewpoint is real, and hence true, and a pseudo-experience which can be of a hysterical or psychotic nature, in which the Zen student is convinced of having obtained *satori*, while the Zen master has to make it clear that he has not. It is precisely one of the functions of the Zen master to be on guard against his student's confusion of real and imaginary enlightenment.

The full awakening to reality means, again speaking in psychological terms, to have attained a fully "productive orientation." That means not to relate oneself to the world receptively, exploitatively, hoardingly, or in the marketing fashion, but creatively, actively (in Spinoza's sense). In the state of full productiveness there are no veils which separate me from the "not me." The object is not an object any more; it does not stand against me, but is with me. The rose I see is not an object for my thought, in the manner that when I say "I see a

27 Foreword to Suzuki, *Introduction to Zen Buddhism*, p. 15.

rose" I only state that the object, a rose, falls under the category "rose," but in the manner that "a rose is a rose is a rose." The state of productiveness is at the same time the state of highest objectivity; I see the object without distortions by my greed and fear. I see it as it or he is, not as I wish it or him to be or not to be. In this mode of perception there are no parataxic distortions. There is complete aliveness, and the synthesis is of subjectivity-objectivity. *I* experience intensely— yet the object is left to be what it is. I bring it to life—and it brings me to life. *Satori* appears mysterious only to the person who is not aware to what degree his perception of the world is purely mental, or parataxical. If one is aware of this, one is also aware of a different awareness, that which one can also call a fully realistic one. One may have only experienced glimpses of it—yet one can imagine what it is. A little boy studying the piano does not play like a great master. Yet the master's playing is nothing mysterious; it is only the perfection of the rudimentary experience the boy has.

That the undistorted and noncerebral perception of reality is an essential element of Zen experience is expressed quite clearly in two Zen stories. One is the story of a master's conversation with a monk:

"Do you ever make an effort to get disciplined in the truth?"

"Yes, I do."

"How do you exercise yourself?"

"When I am hungry, I eat; when I am tired, I sleep."

"This is what everybody does; can they be said to be exercising themselves in the same way as you do?"

"No."

"Why not?"

"Because when they eat, they do not eat, but are thinking of various other things, thereby allowing themselves to be disturbed; when they sleep they do not sleep, but dream of a thousand and one things. This is why they are not like myself." [28]

The story hardly needs any explanation. The average person, driven by insecurity, greed, fear, is constantly enmeshed in a world of phantasies (not necessarily being aware of it) in which he clothes the world in qualities which he projects into it, but which are not there. This was true at the period when this conversation took place; how much more is it true today, when almost everybody sees, hears, feels, and tastes with his thoughts, rather than with those powers within himself which can see, hear, feel, and taste.

The other, equally revealing, statement is that of a Zen master who said: "Before I was enlightened the rivers were rivers and the mountains were mountains. When I began to be enlightened the rivers were not rivers any more and the mountains were not mountains. Now, since I am enlightened, the rivers are rivers again and the mountains are mountains." Again we see the new approach to reality. The average person is like the man in Plato's cave, seeing only the shadows and mistaking them for the substance. Once he has recognized this error, he knows only that the shadows are *not* the substance. But when he becomes enlightened, he has left the cave and its darkness for the light: there he sees the substance and not the shadows. He is awake. As long as he is in the dark, he cannot understand the light (as the Bible says: "A light shines in the darkness and the darkness understandeth not"). Once he be out of the darkness, he understands the difference between how he saw the world as shadows and how he sees it now, as reality.

Zen is aimed at the knowledge of one's own nature. It searches to "know thyself." But this knowledge is not the "scientific" knowledge of the modern psychologist, the knowledge of the knower-intellect who knows himself as object; knowledge of self in Zen is knowledge which is not intellectual, which is non-alienated, it is full experience in which knower and known become one. As Suzuki has put it: "The basic idea of Zen is to come in touch with the inner workings of one's being, and to do this in the most direct way possible, without resorting to anything external or super-added." [29]

This insight into one's own nature is not an intellectual one, standing outside, but an experiential one, being inside, as it were. This difference between intellectual and experiential knowledge is of central importance for Zen and, at the same time, constitutes one of the basic difficulties the Western student has in trying to understand Zen. The West, for two thousand years (and with only few exceptions, such as the mystics)

[29] *Ibid.*, p. 44.

has believed that a final answer to the problem of existence can be given in *thought;* the "right answer" in religion and in philosophy is of paramount importance. By this insistence the way was prepared for the flourishing of the natural sciences. Here the right thought, while not giving a final answer to the problem of existence, is inherent in the method and necessary for the application of the thought to practice, that is, for technique. Zen, on the other hand, is based on the premise that the ultimate answer to life can not be given in thought. "The intellectual groove of 'yes' and 'no' is quite accommodating when things run their regular course; but as soon as the ultimate question of life comes up, the intellect fails to answer satisfactorily." [30] For this very reason, the experience of *satori* can never be conveyed intellectually. It is "an experience which no amount of explanation and argument can make communicable to others, unless the latter themselves had it previously. If *satori* is amenable to analysis in the sense that by so doing it becomes perfectly clear to another who has never had it, that *satori* will not be *satori*. For a *satori* turned into a concept ceases to be itself; and there will no more be a Zen experience." [31]

It is not only that the final answer to life can not be given by any intellectual formulation; in order to arrive at enlightenment, one has to do away with the many constructs of the mind, which impede true insight. "Zen wants one's mind free and unobstructed; even the idea of oneness and allness is a stumbling block and a strangling snare which threatens the original freedom of the spirit." [32] As a further consequence, the concept of participation or empathy, so emphasized by Western psychologists, is unacceptable to Zen thought. "The idea of participation or empathy is an intellectual interpretation of primary experience, while as far as the experience itself is concerned, there is no room for any sort of dichotomy. The intellect, however, obtrudes itself and breaks up the experience in order to make it amenable to intellectual treatment, which means a discrimination or bifurcation. The original feeling of identity is then lost and intellect is allowed to have its character-

[30] *Ibid.,* p. 67.
[31] *Ibid.,* p. 92.
[32] *Ibid.,* p. 41.

istic way of breaking up reality into pieces. Participation or empathy is the result of intellectualization. The philosopher who has no original experience is apt to indulge in it." [33]

Not only intellect, but any authoritative concept or figure, restricts the spontaneity of experience; thus Zen "does not attach any intrinsic importance to the sacred sutras or to their exegesis by the wise and learned. Personal experience is strongly acting against authority and objective revelation. . . ." [34] In Zen God is neither denied nor insisted upon. "Zen wants absolute freedom, even from God." [35] It wants the same freedom, even, from Buddha; hence the Zen saying, "Cleanse your mouth when you utter the word Buddha."

In accordance with Zen's attitude towards intellectual insight, its aim of teaching is not as in the West an ever-increasing subtlety of logical thinking, but its method "consists in putting one in a dilemma, out of which one must contrive to escape not through logic indeed but through a mind of higher order." [36] Accordingly the teacher is not a teacher in the Western sense. He is a master, inasmuch as he has mastered his own mind, and hence is capable of conveying to the student the only thing that can be conveyed: his existence. "With all that the master can do, he is helpless to make the disciple take hold of the thing, unless the latter is fully prepared for it. . . . The taking hold of the ultimate reality is to be done by oneself." [37]

The attitude of the Zen master to his student is bewildering to the modern Western reader who is caught in the alternative between an irrational authority which limits freedom and exploits its object, and a laissez-faire absence of any authority. Zen represents another form of authority, that of "rational authority." The master does not call the student; he wants nothing from him, not even that he becomes enlightened; the student comes of his own free will, and he goes of his own free will. But inasmuch as he wants to learn from the master, the fact has to be recognized that the master is a master, that is, that the master knows what the student wants to know, and

[33] D. T. Suzuki, *Mysticism, Christian and Buddhist,* World Perspective Series, ed. R. N. Anshen (Harper, New York, 1957), p. 105.
[34] D. T. Suzuki, *Introduction to Zen Buddhism,* p. 34.
[35] *Ibid.,* p. 97.
[36] *Ibid.,* p. 40.
[37] D. T. Suzuki, *Zen Buddhism,* p. 96.

does not yet know. For the master "there is nothing to explain by means of words, there is nothing to be given out as a holy doctrine. Thirty blows whether you affirm or negate. Do not remain silent, nor be discursive." [38] The Zen master is characterized at the same time by the complete lack of irrational authority and by the equally strong affirmation of that undemanding authority, the source of which is genuine experience.

Zen can not possibly be understood unless one takes into consideration the idea that the accomplishment of true insight is indissolubly connected with a change in character. Here Zen is rooted in Buddhist thinking, for which characterological transformation is a condition for salvation. Greed for possession, as for anything else, self-conceit and self-glorification are to be left behind. The attitude towards the past is one of gratitude, towards the present, of service, and towards the future, of responsibility. To live in Zen "means to treat yourself and the world in the most appreciative and reverential frame of mind," an attitude which is the basis of "secret virtue, a very characteristic feature of Zen discipline. It means not to waste natural resources; it means to make full use, economic and moral, of everything that comes your way."

As positive aim, the ethical goal of Zen is to achieve "complete security and fearlessness," to move from bondage to freedom. "Zen is a matter of character and not of the intellect, which means that Zen grows out of the will as the first principle of life." [39]

VI. DE-REPRESSION AND ENLIGHTENMENT

What follows from our discussion of psychoanalysis [40] and Zen as to the relationship between the two?

The reader must have been struck by now by the fact that the assumption of incompatibility between Zen Buddhism and psychoanalysis results only from a superficial view of both. Quite to the contrary, the affinity between both seems to be

---

[38] Suzuki, *Introduction to Zen Buddhism,* p. 49.

[39] *Ibid.,* p. 131.

[40] When I speak in this chapter of "psychoanalysis," I refer to humanistic psychoanalysis as a development from Freudian analysis, yet including those aspects of Freudian analysis which are at the root of this development.

much more striking. This chapter is devoted to a detailed elucidation of this affinity.

Let us begin with Dr. Suzuki's statements, quoted earlier, about the aim of Zen. "Zen in its essence is the art of seeing into the nature of one's being, and it points the way from bondage to freedom. . . . We can say that Zen liberates all the energies properly and naturally stored in each of us, which are in ordinary circumstances cramped and distorted so that they find no adequate channel for activity. . . . It is the object of Zen, therefore, to save us from going crazy or being crippled. This is what I mean by freedom, giving free play to all the creative and benevolent impulses inherently lying in our hearts. Generally, we are blind to this fact, that we are in possession of all the necessary faculties that will make us happy and loving towards one another."

This description of Zen's aim could be applied without change as a description of what psychoanalysis aspires to achieve; insight into one's own nature, the achievement of freedom, happiness and love, liberation of energy, salvation from being insane or crippled.

This last statement, that we are confronted with the alternative between enlightenment and insanity, may sound startling, but in my opinion is born out by the observable facts. While psychiatry is concerned with the question of why *some* people become insane, the real question is why *most* people do *not* become insane. Considering man's position in the world, his separateness, aloneness, powerlessness, and his awareness of this, one would expect this burden to be more than he can bear, so that he would, quite literally, "go to pieces" under the strain. Most people avoid this outcome by compensatory mechanisms like the overriding routine of life, conformity with the herd, the search for power, prestige, and money, dependence on idols—shared with others in religious cults—a self-sacrificing masochistic life, narcissistic inflation—in short, by becoming crippled. All these compensatory mechanisms can maintain sanity, provided they work, up to a point. The only fundamental solution which truly overcomes potential insanity is the full, productive response to the world which in its highest form is enlightenment.

Before we arrive at the central issue of the connection between psychoanalysis and Zen I want to consider some more peripheral affinities:

First to be mentioned is the ethical orientation common to Zen and to psychoanalysis. A condition for achieving the aim of Zen is the overcoming of greed, be it greed for possession or glory, or any other form of greed ("coveting," in the Old Testament sense). This is exactly what the aim of psychoanalysis is. In his theory of the libido evolution from the oral receptive, through the oral sadistic, the anal, to the genital level, Freud implicitly stated that the healthy character develops from the greedy, cruel, stingy, into an active, independent orientation. In my own terminology, which follows Freud's clinical observations, I have made this value element more explicit by speaking about evolution from the receptive, through the exploitative, hoarding, marketing, to the productive orientation.[41] Whatever terminology one uses, the essential point is that, in the psychoanalytic concept, greed is a pathological phenomenon; it exists where a person has not developed his active, productive capacities. Yet neither psychoanalysis nor Zen is *primarily* an ethical system. The aim of Zen transcends the goal of ethical behavior, and so does psychoanalysis. It might be said that both systems assume that the achievement of their aim brings with it an ethical transformation, the overcoming of greed and the capacity for love and compassion. They do not tend to make a man lead a virtuous life by the suppression of the "evil" desire, but they expect that the evil desire will melt away and disappear under the light and warmth of enlarged consciousness. But whatever the causal connection between enlightenment and ethical transformation may be, it would be a fundamental error to believe that the goal of Zen can be separated from the aim of overcoming greed, self glorification, and folly, or that *satori* can be achieved without achieving humility, love, and compassion. It would be equally a mistake to assume that the aim of psychoanalysis is achieved unless a similar transformation in the person's character occurs. A person who has reached the productive level is not greedy, and at the same time he has overcome his grandiosity and the fictions of ominiscience and omipotence; he is humble and sees himself as he is. Both Zen and psychoanalysis aim at something

[41] *Man for Himself* (New York, Rinehart, 1947), Chapter III.

transcending ethics, yet their aim can not be accomplished
unless an ethical transformation takes place.

Another element common to both systems is their insistence
on independence from any kind of authority. This is Freud's
main reason for criticizing religion. He saw as the essence of
religion the illusion of substituting the dependence on God for
the original dependence on a helping and punishing father.
In the belief in God, man, according to Freud, continues his
infantile dependence, rather than matures, which means to rely
only on his own strength. What would Freud have said to a
"religion" which says: "When you have mentioned Buddha's
name, wash your mouth!" What would he have said to a
religion in which there is no God, no irrational authority of
any kind, whose main goal is exactly that of liberating man
from all dependence, activating him, showing him that he, and
nobody else, bears the responsibility for his fate?

Yet, it might be asked, does this anti-authoritarian attitude
not contradict the significance of the person of the master in
Zen, and of the analyst in psychoanalysis? Again, this question
points to an element in which there is a profound connection
between Zen and psychoanalysis. In both systems a guide is
needed, one who has himself gone through the experience the
patient (student) under his care is to achieve. Does this mean
that the student becomes dependent on the master (or psychoanalyst) and that hence the master's words constitute truth for
him? Undoubtedly, psychoanalysts deal with the *fact* of such
dependence (transference) and recognize the powerful influence
which it can have. But the aim of psychoanalysis is to understand and eventually to dissolve this tie, and instead to bring
the patient to a point where he has acquired full freedom from
the analyst, because he has experienced in himself that which
was unconscious and has reintegrated it into his consciousness.
The Zen master—and the same can be said of the psychoanalyst
—knows more, and hence can have conviction in his judgment,
but that does not at all mean that he imposes his judgment on
the student. He has not called the student, and he does not
prevent him from leaving him. If the student voluntarily comes
to him and wants his guidance in walking the steep path to
enlightenment, the master is willing to guide him, but only
under one condition: that the student understands that, much

as the master wants to help him, the student must look after himself. None of us can save anybody else's soul. One can only save oneself. All the master can do is to play the role of a midwife, of a guide in the mountains. As one master said, "I really have nothing to impart to you and if I tried to do so, you might have occasion to make me an object of ridicule. Besides, whatever I can tell you is my own, and can never be yours."

A very striking and concrete illustration of the Zen master's attitude is to be found in Herrigel's book on the art of archery.[42] The Zen master insists upon his rational authority, that is to say, that he knows better how to achieve the art of archery, and therefore must stress a certain way of learning it, but he does not want any irrational authority, any power over the student, the continued dependence of the student on the master. On the contrary, once the student has become a master himself, he goes his own way, and all that the master expects from him is a picture from time to time which will show him how the student is doing. It might be said that the Zen master loves his students. His love is one of realism and maturity, of making every effort to help the student in achieving his aim, and yet of knowing that nothing the master does can solve the problem *for* the student, can achieve the aim for him. This love of the Zen master is non-sentimental, realistic love, a love which accepts the reality of human fate in which none of us can save the other, and yet in which we must never cease to make every effort to give help so that another can save himself. Any love which does not know this limitation, and claims to be able to "save" another soul, is one which has not rid itself of grandiosity and ambition.

Further proof that what has been said about the Zen Master in principle holds true (or should hold true) for the psycho-analyst is hardly necessary. Freud thought that the patient's independence of the analyst could best be established by a mirror-like, impersonal attitude on the part of the analyst. But analysts like Ferenczi, Sullivan, myself, and others, who stress the need for relatedness between analysts and patient as a con-dition for understanding, would entirely agree that this related-

[42] Eugen Herrigel, *Zen in the Art of Archery* (New York, Pantheon Books, 1953).

ness must be free from all sentimentality, unrealistic distortions, and, especially, from any—even the most subtle and indirect—interference of the analyst in the life of the patient, not even that of the demand that the patient gets well. If the patient wants to get well and to change, that is fine, and the analyst is willing to help him. If his resistance to change is too great, this is not the analyst's responsibility. All his responsibility lies in lending the best of his knowledge and effort, of giving himself to the patient in search of the aim the patient seeks him out for.

Related to the attitude of the analyst is another affinity between Zen Buddhism and psychoanalysis. The "teaching" method of Zen is to drive the student into a corner, as it were. The koan makes it impossible for the student to seek refuge in intellectual thought; the koan is like a barrier which makes further flight impossible. The analyst does—or should do—something similar. He must avoid the error of feeding the patient with interpretations and explanations which only prevent the patient from making the jump from thinking into experiencing. On the contrary, he must take away one rationalization after another, one crutch after another, until the patient cannot escape any longer, and instead breaks through the fictions which fill his mind and experiences reality—that is, becomes conscious of something he was not conscious of before. This process often produces a good deal of anxiety, and sometimes the anxiety would prevent the break-through, were it not for the reassuring pressence of the analyst. But this reassurance is one of "being there," not one of words which tend to inhibit the patient from experiencing what only he can experience.

Our discussion thus far has dealt with tangential points of similarity or affinity between Zen Buddhism and psychoanalysis. But no such comparison can be satisfactory unless it deals squarely with the main issue of Zen, which is enlightenment, and the main issue of psychoanalysis, which is the overcoming of repressedness, the transformation of the unconscious into consciousness.

Let us sum up what has been said about this problem as far as psychoanalysis is concerned. The aim of psychoanalysis is to make the unconscious conscious. However, to speak of "the" conscious and "the" unconscious means to take words for realities. We must stick to the fact that conscious and unconscious refer to functions, not to places or contents. Properly speaking, then, we can talk only of states of various degrees of repressedness, that is, a state in which only those experiences are permitted to come to awareness which can penetrate through the social filter of language, logic, and content. To the degree to which I can rid myself of this filter and can experience myself as the universal man, that is, to the degree to which repressedness diminishes, I am in touch with the deepest sources within myself, and that means with all of humanity. If all repressedness has been lifted, there is no more unconscious as against conscious; there is direct, immediate experience; inasmuch as I am not a stranger to myself, no one and nothing is a stranger to me. Furthermore, to the degree to which part of me is alienated from myself, and my "unconscious" is separated from my conscious (that is I, the whole man, am separated from the I, the social man), my grasp of the world is falsified in several ways. First, in the way of parataxic distortions (transference); I experience the other person not with my total self, but with my split, childish self, and thus another person is experienced as a significant person of one's childhood, and not as the person he really is.

Secondly, man in the state of repressedness experiences the world with a false consciousness. He does not see what exists, but he puts his thought image into things, and sees them in the light of his thought images and fantasies, rather than in their reality. It is the thought image, the distorting veil, that creates his passions, his anxieties. Eventually, the repressed man, instead of experiencing things and persons, experiences by *cerebration*. He is under the illusion of being in touch with the *world*, while he is only in touch with *words*. Parataxic distortion, false consciousness, and cerebration are not strictly separate ways of unreality; they are, rather, different and yet overlapping aspects of the same phenomenon of unreality which exists as long as the universal man is separated from the social man. We only describe the same phenomenon in a different way by saying that the person who lives in the state of repressedness is the alienated person. He projects his own feelings and ideas on objects, and then does not experience himself as the subject of his feelings, but is ruled by the objects which are charged with his feelings.

The opposite of the alienated, distorted, parataxic, false, cerebrated experience, is the immediate, direct, total grasp of the world which we see in the infant and child before the power of education changes this form of experience. For the new-born infant there is as yet no separation between the me and the not-me. This separation gradually takes place, and the final achievement is expressed by the fact that the child can say "I." But still the child's grasp of the world remains relatively immediate and direct. When the child plays with a ball, it really sees the ball moving, it is fully *in* this experience, and that is why it is an experience which can be repeated without end, and with a never ceasing joy. The adult also believes that he sees the ball rolling. That is of course true, inasmuch as he sees that the object-ball is rolling on the object-floor. But he does not really *see* the rolling. He *thinks* the rolling ball on the surface. When he says "the ball rolls," he actually confirms only (a) his knowledge that the round object over there is called a ball and (b) his knowledge that round objects roll on a smooth surface when given a push. His eyes operate with the end of proving his knowledge, and thus making him secure in the world.

The state of non-repressedness is a state in which one acquires again the immediate, undistorted grasp of reality, the simpleness and spontaneity of the child; yet, *after* having gone through the process of alienation, of development of one's intellect, non-repressedness is return to innocence on a higher level; this return to innocence is possible only after one has lost one's innocence.

This whole idea has found a clear expression in the Old Testament, in the story of the Fall, and in the prophetic concept of the Messiah. Man, in the biblical story, finds himself in a state of undifferentiated unity in the Garden of Eden. There is no consciousness, no differentiation, no choice, no freedom, no sin. He is part of nature, and he is not aware of any distance between himself and nature. This state of primordial, pre-individual unity is disrupted by the first act of choice, which is at the same time the first act of disobedience and of freedom. The act brings about the emergence of consciousness. Man is aware of himself as he, of his separateness from Eve-the woman, and from nature, animals, and the earth. When he experiences this separateness he feels ashamed—as we all still feel ashamed (though unconsciously) when we experience the separateness from our fellowman. He leaves the Garden of Eden, and this is the beginning of human history. He can not return to the original state of harmony yet he can strive for a new state of harmony by developing his reason, his objectivity, his conscience, and his love fully, so that, as the prophets express it, the "earth is full of the knowledge of God as the ocean is full of water." History, in the Messianic concept, is the place in which there will occur this development from pre-individual, pre-conscious harmony to a new harmony, a harmony based on the completion and perfection of the development of reason. This new state of harmony is called the Messianic time in which the conflict between man and nature, man and man, will have disappeared, in which the desert will become a fruitful valley, in which the lamb and the wolf will rest side by side, and in which swords will be transformed into ploughshares. The Messianic time is the time of the Garden of Eden, and yet it is its opposite. It is oneness, immediacy, entirety, but of the fully developed man who has become a child again, yet has outgrown being a child.

The same idea is expressed in the New Testament: "Truly, I say to you, whosoever does not receive the Kingdom of God like a child shall not enter it." [43] The meaning is clear: we have to become children again, to experience the unalienated, creative grasp of the world; but in becoming children again we are at the same time not children, but fully developed adults. Then, indeed, we have the experience which the New Testament describes like this: "For now we see in a mirror dimly, but then face to face. Now I know in part; then I shall understand fully even as I have been fully understood." [44]

To "become conscious of the unconscious" means to overcome repressedness and alienation from myself, and hence from the stranger. It means to wake up, to shed illusions, fictions, and lies, to see reality as it is. The man who wakes up is the liberated man, the man whose freedom cannot be restricted

43 Luke 18: 17.
44 I Corinthians 13: 11.

either by others or by himself. The process of becoming aware of that which one was not aware of constitutes the inner revolution of man. It is the true awakening which is at the root of both creative intellecutal thought and intuitive immediate grasp. To lie is possible only in a state of alienation, where reality is not experienced except as a thought. In the state of being open to reality which exists in being awakened, to lie is impossible because the lie would melt under the strength of experiencing fully. In the last analysis, to make the unconscious conscious means to live in truth. Reality has ceased to be alienated; I am open to it; I let it be; hence my responses to it are "true."

This aim of the immediate, full grasp of the world is the aim of Zen. Since Dr. Suzuki has written a chapter dealing with the unconscious in this book, I can refer to his discussion, and thus try to clarify further the connection between the psychoanalytic and the Zen concepts.

First of all, I should like to point again to the terminological difficulty which, I believe, unnecessarily complicates matters; the use of *the* conscious and *the* unconscious, instead of the functional term of greater or lesser awareness of experience in the total man. I believe that, if we free our discussion from these terminological obstacles, we can recognize more readily the connection between the true meaning of making the unconscious conscious and the idea of enlightenment.

"The Zen approach is to enter right into the object itself and see it, as it were, from the inside." [45] This immediate grasp of reality "may also be called conative or creative." [46] Suzuki then speaks of this source of creativity as of "Zen's unconscious" and continues by saying that "the unconscious is something to feel, not in its ordinary sense, but in what I would call the most primary or fundamental sense." [47] The formulation speaks here of the unconscious as of a realm within the personality and transcending it, and, as Suzuki goes on to say, "the feeling of the unconscious is . . . basic [and] primary." [48] Translating this into functional terms I would not speak of feeling

45 D. T. Suzuki, "Lectures on Zen Buddhism," *supra*, p. 11.
46 *Ibid.*, p. 12.
47 *Ibid.*, p. 14.
48 *Idem.*

"the" unconscious, but rather of being aware of a deeper and not conventionalized area of experience, or to put it differently, lessening the degree of repressedness, and thus reducing the parataxic distortion, image projections, and cerebration of reality. When Suzuki speaks of the Zen-man as being "in direct communion with the great unconscious," [49] I would prefer the formulation: being aware of his own reality, and of the reality of the world in its full depth and without veils. A little later Suzuki uses the same functional language when he states: "In fact, it [the unconscious] is, on the contrary, the most intimate thing to us and it is just because of this intimacy that it is difficult to take hold of, in the same way as the eye can not see itself. *To become,* therefore, *conscious of the unconscious requires a special training on the part of consciousness.*" [50] Here Suzuki chooses a formulation which would be exactly the one chosen from the psychoanalytic standpoint: the aim is to become conscious of the unconscious, and in order to achieve this aim a special training on the part of consciousness is necessary. Does this imply that Zen and psychoanalysis have the same aim, and that they differ only in the training of the consciousness they have developed?

Before we return to this point, I should like to discuss a few other points which need to be clarified.

Dr. Suzuki, in his discussion, refers to the same problem which I mentioned in the discussion of the psychoanalytic concept above, that of knowledge vs. the state of innocence. What is called in biblical terms the loss of innocence, through the acquisition of knowledge, is called in Zen and in Buddhism generally "the 'affective contamination *(klesha)*' or 'the interference of the conscious mind predominated by intellection *(vijñāna).*'" The term intellection raises a very important problem. Is intellection the same as consciousness? In this case, making the unconscious conscious would imply the furthering of intellection and indeed lead to an aim exactly opposite to Zen's. If this were so, then indeed the aim of psychoanalysis and of Zen would be diametrically opposed, the one striving for more intellection, the other striving for the overcoming of intellection.

---

49 *Ibid.,* p. 16.
50 *Ibid.,* p. 18. (My italics—E. F.)

It must be admitted that Freud, in the earlier years of his work, when he still believed that the proper information given the patient by the psychoanalyst was enough to cure him, had a concept of intellection as the goal of psychoanalysis; it must be admitted further that many analysts in practice have still not emerged from this concept of intellection, and that Freud never expressed himself with full clarity on the difference between intellection and the affective, total experience which occurs in genuine "working through." Yet, it is precisely this experimental and not-intellectual insight which constitutes the aim of psychoanalysis. As I stated before, to be aware of my breathing does not mean *to think about* my breathing. To be aware of the movement of my hand does not mean to think about it. On the contrary, once I *think about* my breathing or the movement of my hand, I am not any more aware of my breathing or of the movement of my hand. The same holds true of my awareness of a flower or a person, of my experience of joy, love, or peace. It is characteristic of all true insight in psychoanalysis that it cannot be formulated in thought, while it is characteristic of all bad analysis that "insight" is formulated in complicated theories which have nothing to do with immediate experience. The authentic psychoanalytic insight is sudden; it arrives without being forced or even being premeditated. It starts not in our brain but, to use a Japanese image, in our belly. It can not be adequately formulated in words and it eludes one if one tries to do so; yet it is real and conscious, and leaves the person who experiences it a changed person.

The immediate grasp of the world by the infant is one before consciousness, objectivity, and a sense of reality as separate from self are fully developed. In this state "the unconscious is an instinctive one, it does not go beyond that of animals and infants. It cannot be that of the mature man." [51] During the emergence from primitive unconsciousness to self-consciousness, the world is experienced as an alienated one on the basis of the split between subject and object, of separation between the universal man and the social man, between unconscious and consciousness. To the degree, however, to which consciousness is trained to open itself, to loosen the threefold filter, the discrepancy between consciousness and unconsciousness disap-

[51] *Ibid.*, p. 19.

pears. When it has fully disappeared there is direct, unreflected, conscious experience, precisely the kind of experience which exists without intellection and reflection. This knowledge is what Spinoza called the highest form of knowledge, *intuition;* the knowledge which Suzuki describes as the approach which "is to enter right into the object itself and see it, as it were, from the inside"; it is the conative or creative way of seeing reality. In this experience of the immediate, unreflected grasp, man becomes the "creative artist of life" which we all are and yet have forgotten that we are. "To such [creative artist of life] his every deed expresses originality, creativity, his living personality. There is no conventionality, no conformity, no inhibitory motivation. . . . He has no self encased in his fragmentary, limited, restrained egocentric existence. He is gone out of this prison." [52]

The "mature man," if he has cleansed himself of "affective contamination" and the interference of intellection, can realize "a life of freedom and spontaneity where such disturbing feelings as fear, anxiety, or insecurity have no room to assail him." [53] What Suzuki says here of the liberating function of this achievement is, indeed, what from the psychoanalytic standpoint would be said of the expected effect of full insight.

There remains a question of terminology which I want to mention only briefly since, like all terminological questions, it is not of great importance. I mentioned before that Suzuki speaks of the training of consciousness; but in other places he speaks of the *"trained unconscious* in which all the conscious experiences he has gone through since infancy are incorporated as constituting his whole being." [54] One might find a contradiction in the use at one time of the "trained consciousness" and at another time of the "trained unconsciousness." But actually I do not believe that we deal here with a contradiction at all. In the process of making the unconscious conscious, of arriving at the full and hence unreflected reality of experience, both the conscious and the unconscious must be trained. The conscious must be trained to loosen its reliance on the conventional filter, while the unconscious must be trained to

52 *Ibid.,* p. 16.
53 *Ibid.,* p. 20.
54 *Ibid.,* p. 19. (My italics—E. F.)

emerge from its secret, separate existence, into the light. But in reality, speaking of the training of consciousness and unconsciousness means using metaphors. Neither the unconscious nor the conscious need to be trained (since there is neither a conscious nor an unconscious), but *man* must be trained to drop his repressedness and to experience reality fully, clearly, in all awareness, and yet without intellectual reflection, except where intellectual reflection is wanted or necessary, as in science and in practical occupations.

Suzuki suggests calling this unconscious the Cosmic Unconscious. There is, of course, no valid argument against this terminology, provided it is explained as clearly as in Suzuki's text. Nevertheless, I would prefer to use the term "Cosmic Consciousness," which Bucke used to denote a new, emerging form of consciousness.[55] I would prefer this term because if, and to the degree to which, the unconscious becomes conscious, it ceases to be unconscious (always keeping in mind that it does not become reflective intellection). The cosmic unconsciousness is the unconscious only as long as we are separated from it, that is, as long as we are unconscious of reality. To the degree to which we awaken and are in touch with reality, there is nothing we are unconscious of. It must be added that by using the term *Cosmic Consciousness,* rather than *conscious,* reference is made to the function of awareness rather than to a place within the personality.

Where does this whole discussion lead us with regard to the relationship between Zen Buddhism and psychoanalysis?

The aim of Zen is enlightenment: the immediate, unreflected grasp of reality, without affective contamination and intellec-

---

[55] Richard R. Bucke, *Cosmic Consciousness, A Study in the Evolution of the Human Mind* (Innes & Sons, 1901; New York, Dutton, 1923, 17th ed., 1954). It should be mentioned, though only in passing, that Bucke's book is perhaps the book most germane to the topic of this article. Bucke, a psychiatrist of great knowledge and experience, a socialist with a profound belief in the necessity and possibility of a socialist society which "will abolish individual ownership and rid the earth at once of two immense evils—riches and poverty," develops in this book a hypothesis of the evolution of human consciousness. According to his hypothesis, man has progressed from animal "simple consciousness" to human self-consciousness, and is now on the threshold of developing Cosmic Consciousness, a revolutionary event which has already occurred in a number of extraordinary personalities in the last two thousand years. What Bucke describes as cosmic consciousness is, in my opinion, precisely the experience which is called *satori* in Zen Buddhism.

tualization, the realization of the relation of myself to the Universe. This new experience is a repetition of the pre-intellectual, immediate grasp of the child, but on a new level, that of the full development of man's reason, objectivity, individuality. While the child's experience, that of immediacy and oneness, lies *before* the experience of alienation and the subject-object split, the enlightenment experience lies after it.

The aim of psychoanalysis, as formulated by Freud, is that of making the unconscious conscious, of replacing Id by Ego. To be sure, the content of the unconscious to be discovered was limited to a small sector of the personality, to those instinctual drives which were alive in early childhood, but which were subject to amnesia. To lift these out of the state of repression was the aim of the analytic technique. Furthermore, the sector to be uncovered, quite aside from Freud's theoretical premises, was determined by the therapeutic need to cure a particular symptom. There was little interest in recovering unconsciousness outside of the sector related to the symptom formation. Slowly the introduction of the concept of the death instinct and eros and the development of the Ego aspects in recent years have brought about a certain broadening of the Freudian concepts of the contents of the unconscious. The non-Freudian schools greatly widened the sector of the unconscious to be uncovered. Most radically Jung, but also Adler, Rank, and the other more recent so-called neo-Freudian authors have contributed to this extension. But (with the exception of Jung), in spite of such a widening, the extent of the sector to be uncovered has remained determined by the therapeutic aim of curing this or that symptom; or this or that neurotic character trait. It has not encompassed the whole person.

However, if one follows the original aim of Freud, that of making the unconscious conscious, to its last consequences, one must free it from the limitations imposed on it by Freud's own instinctual orientation, and by the immediate task of curing symptoms. If one pursues the aim of the full recovery of the unconscious, then this task is not restricted to the instincts, nor to other limited sectors of experience, but to the total experience of the total man; then the aim becomes that of overcoming alienation, and of the subject-object split in perceiving the world; then the uncovering of the unconscious means the overcoming of affective contamination and cerebration; it means the de-repression, the abolition of the split within myself between the universal man and the social man; it means the disappearance of the polarity of conscious vs. unconscious; it means arriving at the state of the immediate grasp of reality, without distortion and without interference by intellectual reflection; it means overcoming of the craving to hold on to the ego, to worship it; it means giving up the illusion of an indestructible separate ego, which is to be enlarged, preserved and as the Egyptian pharaohs hoped to preserve themselves as mummies for eternity. To be conscious of the unconscious means to be open, responding, to *have* nothing and to *be*.

This aim of the full recovery of unconsciousness by consciousness is quite obviously much more radical than the general psychoanalytic aim. The reasons for this are easy to see. To achieve this total aim requires an effort far beyond the effort most persons in the West are willing to make. But quite aside from this question of effort, even the visualization of this aim is possible only under certain conditions. First of all, this radical aim can be envisaged only from the point of view of a certain philosophical position. There is no need to describe this position in detail. Suffice it to say that it is one in which not the negative aim of the absence of sickness, but the positive one of the presence of well-being is aimed at, and that well-being is conceived in terms of full union, the immediate and uncontaminated grasp of the world. This aim could not be better described than has been done by Suzuki in terms of "the art of living." One must keep in mind that any such concept as the art of living grows from the soil of a spiritual humanistic orientation, as it underlies the teaching of Buddha, of the prophets, of Jesus, of Meister Eckhart, or of men such as Blake, Walt Whitman, or Bucke. Unless it is seen in this context, the concept of "the art of living" loses all that is specific, and deteriorates into a concept that goes today under the name of "happiness." It must also not be forgotten that this orientation includes an ethical aim. While Zen transcends ethics, it includes the basic ethical aims of Buddhism, which are essentially the same as those of all humanistic teaching. The achievement of the aim of Zen, as Suzuki has made very clear in the lectures in this book, implies the overcoming of greed in all forms, whether it is the greed for possession, for fame, or for affection; it implies overcoming narcissistic self-glorification and the illusion of omnipotence. It implies, furthermore, the overcoming of the desire to submit to an authority who solves one's own problem of existence. The person who only wants to use the discovery of the unconscious to be cured of sickness will, of course, not even attempt to achieve the radical aim which lies in the overcoming of repressedness.

But it would be a mistake to believe that the radical aim of the de-repression has no connection with a therapeutic aim. Just as one has recognized that the cure of a symptom and the prevention of future symptom formations is not possible without the analysis and change of the character, one must also recognize that the change of this or that neurotic character trait is not possible without pursuing the more radical aim of a complete transformation of the person. It may very well be that the relatively disappointing results of character analysis (which have never been expressed more honestly than by Freud in his "Analysis, Terminable or Interminable?") are due precisely to the fact that the aims for the cure of the neurotic character were not radical enough; that well-being, freedom from anxiety and insecurity, can be achieved only if the limited aim is transcended, that is, if one realizes that the limited, therapeutic aim cannot be achieved as long as it remains limited and does not become part of a wider, humanistic frame of reference. Perhaps the limited aim can be achieved with more limited and less time-consuming methods, while the time and energy consumed in the long analytic process are used fruitfully only for the radical aim of "transformation" rather than the narrow one of "reform." This proposition might be strengthened by referring to a statement made above. Man, as long as he has not reached the creative relatedness of which *satori* is the fullest achievement, at best compensates for inherent potential depression by routine, idolatry, destructiveness, greed for property or fame, etc. When any of these compensations break down, his sanity is threatened. The cure of the potential insanity lies only in the change in attitude from split and alienation to the creative, immediate grasp of and response to the world. If psychoanalysis can help in this way, it can help to achieve true mental health; if it cannot, it will only help to improve compensatory mechanisms. To put it still differently: somebody may be "cured" of a symptom, but he can not be "cured" of a character neurosis. Man is not a thing,[56] man is not a "case," and the analyst does not cure anybody by treating him as an object. Rather, the analyst can only help a man to wake up, in a process in which the analyst is engaged with the "patient" in the process of their understanding each other, which means experiencing their oneness.

In stating all this, however, we must be prepared to be confronted with an objection. If, as I said above, the achievement of the full consciousness of the unconscious is as radical and difficult an aim as enlightenment, does it make any sense to discuss this radical aim as something which has any general application? Is it not purely speculative to raise seriously the question that only this radical aim can justify the hopes of psychoanalytic therapy?

If there were only the alternative between full enlightenment and nothing, then indeed this objection would be valid. But this is not so. In Zen there are many stages of enlightenment, of which *satori* is the ultimate and decisive step. But, as far as I understand, value is set on experiences which are steps in the direction of *satori,* although *satori* may never be reached. Dr. Suzuki once illustrated this point in the following way: If one candle is brought into an absolutely dark room, the darkness disappears, and there is light. But if ten or a hundred or a thousand candles are added, the room will become brighter and brighter. Yet the decisive change was brought about by the first candle which penetrated the darkness.[57]

What happens in the analytic process? A person senses for the first time that he is vain, that he is frightened, that he hates, while consciously he had believed himself to be modest, brave, and loving. The new insight may hurt him, but it opens a door; it permits him to stop projecting on others what he represses in himself. He proceeds; he experiences the infant, the child, the adolescent, the criminal, the insane, the saint,

---

[56] Cf. my paper: "The Limitations and Dangers of Psychology," in *Religion and Culture,* ed. by W. Leibrecht. (New York, Harper & Brothers, 1959), pp. 31 ff.

[57] In a personal communication, as I remember.

the artist, the male, *and* the female within himself; he gets more deeply in touch with humanity, with the universal man; he represses less, is freer, has less need to project, to cerebrate; then he may experience for the first time how he sees colors, how he sees a ball roll, how his ears are suddenly fully opened to music, when up to now he only listened *to* it; in sensing his oneness with others, he may have a first glimpse of the illusion that his separate individual ego is some*thing* to hold onto, to cultivate, to save; he will experience the futility of seeking the answer to life by *having* himself, rather than by being and becoming himself. All these are sudden, unexpected experiences with no intellectual content; yet afterwards the person feels freer, stronger, less anxious than he ever felt before.

So far we have spoken about *aims,* and I have proposed that if one carries Freud's principle of the transformation of unconsciousness into consciousness to its ultimate consequences, one approaches the concept of enlightenment. But as to *methods* of achieving this aim, psychoanalysis and Zen are, indeed, entirely different. The method of Zen is, one might say, that of a frontal attack on the alienated way of perception by means of the "sitting," the koan, and the authority of the master. Of course, all this is not a "technique" which can be isolated from the premise of Buddhist thinking, of the behavior and ethical values which are embodied in the master and in the atmosphere of the monastery. It must also be remembered that it is not a "five hour a week" concern, and that by the very fact of coming for instruction in Zen the student has made a most important decision, a decision which is an important part of what goes on afterwards.

The psychoanalytic method is entirely different from the Zen method. It trains consciousness to get hold of the unconscious in a different way. It directs attention to that perception which is distorted; it leads to a recognition of the fiction within oneself; it widens the range of human experience by lifting repressedness. The analytic method is psychological-empirical. It examines the psychic development of a person from childhood on and tries to recover earlier experiences in order to assist the person in experiencing of what is now repressed. It proceeds by uncovering illusions within oneself about the world, step by step, so that parataxic distortions and alienated intellectualizations diminish. By becoming less of a stranger to himself, the person who goes through this process becomes less estranged to the world; because he has opened up communication with the universe within himself, he has opened up communication with the universe outside. False consciousness disappears, and with it the polarity conscious-unconscious. A new realism dawns in which "the mountains are mountains again." The psychoanalytic method is of course only a method, a preparation; but so is the Zen method. By the very fact that it is a method it never guarantees the achievement of the goal. The factors which permit this achievement are deeply rooted in the individual personality, and for all practical purposes we know little of them.

I have suggested that the method of uncovering the unconscious, if carried to its ultimate consequences, may be a step toward enlightenment, provided it is taken within the philosophical context which is most radically and realistically expressed in Zen. But only a great deal of further experience in applying this method will show how far it can lead. The view expressed here implies only a possibility and thus has the character of a hypothesis which is to be tested.

But what can be said with more certainty is that the knowledge of Zen, and a concern with it, can have a most fertile and clarifying influence on the theory and technique of psychoanalysis. Zen, different as it is in its method from psychoanalysis, can sharpen the focus, throw new light on the nature of insight, and heighten the sense of what it is to see, what it is to be creative, what it is to overcome the affective contaminations and false intellectualizations which are the necessary results of experience based on the subject-object split.

In its very radicalism with respect to intellectualization, authority, and the delusion of the ego, in its emphasis on the aim of well-being, Zen thought will deepen and widen the horizon of the psychoanalyst and help him to arrive at a more radical concept of the grasp of reality as the ultimate aim of full, conscious awareness.

If further speculation on the relation between Zen and psychoanalysis is permissible, one might think of the possibility that psychoanalysis may be significant to the student of Zen. I can visualize it as a help in avoiding the danger of a false enlightenment (which is, of course, no enlightenment), one which is purely subjective, based on psychotic or hysterical phenomena, or on a self-induced state of trance. Analytic clarification might help the Zen student to avoid illusions, the absence of which is the very condition of enlightenment.

Whatever the use is that Zen may make of psychoanalysis, from the standpoint of a Western psychoanalyst I express my gratitude for this precious gift of the East, especially to Dr. Suzuki, who has succeeded in expressing it in such a way that none of its essence becomes lost in the attempt to translate Eastern into Western thinking, so that the Westerner, if he takes the trouble, can arrive at an understanding of Zen, as far as it can be arrived at before the goal is reached. How could such understanding be possible, were it not for the fact that "Buddha nature is in all of us," that man and existence, are universal categories, and that the immediate grasp of reality, waking up, and enlightenment, are universal experiences.

THE HUMAN SITUATION
AND ZEN BUDDHISM[1]

By Richard De Martino

My task, in this hour, is to present an overall view of Zen Buddhism with respect to the specific concerns of this conference, namely, depth psychology and psychotherapy. To this end, within the limit of my own unauthoritative understanding, I shall attempt to provide a general consideration of Zen Buddhism in its relation to the human situation.

Human existence is, initially, self-conscious, or, in the designation here to be preferred, ego-conscious existence. Man is not simply born into human existence. The infant is not yet human; the idiot never quite human; the "wolf-child" only quasi-human; the hopeless psychotic perhaps no longer human.

Not that the infant, the idiot, the "wolf-child," or the psychotic is ever sheer animal. The pre-ego-conscious state of the infant, the abortive ego-consciousness of the idiot, the retarded ego-consciousness of the "wolf-child," and the deteriorated ego-consciousness of the psychotic all derive their particular determination from what would be the norm of their developed and unimpaired being. This norm is that ego-consciousness which ordinarily first appears between the ages of two and five in a child born of human parents and reared in

[1] While the responsibility for the position offered must remain solely his own, the writer wishes to acknowledge his profound indebtedness to Professors Reinhold Niebuhr and Paul Tillich, to Dr. Shinichi Hisamatsu, and, above all, to Dr. Daisetz T. Suzuki.

a human society. Foregoing at this time any phenomenological account of its onset and development, let us rather proceed immediately to an analysis of its nature and to an examination of its implications for the human situation.

Ego-consciousness means an ego aware or conscious of itself. Awareness of itself is expressed as affirmation of itself, the "I," or, as I shall continue to call it, the ego. Affirmation of itself involves the individuation of itself, the ego differentiated and discriminated from that which is not itself—"the other," or simply its own negation, "not-I" or "non-ego." Affirmation of itself also entails, however, a bifurcation of itself.

Affirmation of itself includes itself both as affirmer and as affirmed. As affirmer it performs the act of affirming itself. As affirmed it is an existential fact presented to itself. The awareness and affirmation of itself in which it indeed emerges or appears is at once both an act undertaken by the ego and a fact given to the ego. The ego as subject-affirmer is not chronologically prior to itself as object-affirmed. Nor does its individuation precede its bifurcation. Immediately when there is ego-consciousness there is the ego, and immediately when there is the ego it is already object as well as subject, as much imparted to itself as it is the activator of itself. A living, active subject with freedom and responsibility, it is at the same time a passive, given object, destined, determined, and without responsibility. This is the perennial nature and structure of the ego in ego-consciousness. This is the initial situation of man in human existence, a situation which may be characterized as contingent or conditioned subjectivity.

Conditioned subjectivity, although conditioned, is, nonetheless, subjectivity. The rise of ego-consciousness marks the rise of subjectivity. Existence comes to be human existence precisely through subjectivity. As subject the ego is aware of and has itself. Further, as subject, encountering—and acknowledging—the subjectivity of others similarly aware of and having themselves, it can learn to control, discipline, and train itself, and thus to become a centered person. The infant, however, is not yet a person, the idiot never quite a person, the "wolf-child" merely a quasi-person, and the psychotic perhaps no longer a person. As subject the ego, in addition, is aware of and has a world, its world. Moreover, as subject it can, in the

freedom of its subjectivity, ever rise above and transcend itself
and its world in any given aspect. In expression of its inviolable
integrity as subject-person—toward either its world or itself—
it can always finally resist and say, "No!"

Again, as subject the ego can go out of itself and participate
in the subjectivity of the other in friendship, compassion, and
love. Also as subject it can have language and entertain meaning, can question, doubt, and understand, can reflect, evaluate,
and judge, can conceive, fabricate, and use tools, can make and
execute decisions, can work, and can be creative, expressing
itself in or through some object or activity. Indeed, only as
subject can it have an object.

In its subjectivity the ego, thus, has—and can rise above—
itself and its world, can love, can understand, can decide, can
create, and can be productive. This is the greatness of the ego
in ego-consciousness. This is the dignity of man in human
existence.

Yet, just as subject—and this is part of its greatness—the ego
realizes that its subjectivity is a contingent or conditioned
subjectivity. Free, as subject, to transcend any given object
aspect of itself or its world, it has not the freedom, as ego, to
transcend its subject-object structure as such. Even as tran-
scender, it is still linked to that which is transcended. The
ego as subject is forever bound to itself and its world as object.
As subject it activates itself and has its world. As object it is
given to itself in all of its particularity and finitude as part of
the world in which it finds itself. Capable of having an object
solely because it is a subject, it can never be a subject except
insofar as it also is or has an object.

Object-dependent and object-conditioned, the ego is, further,
object-obstructed. In the subjectivity in which it is aware of
and has itself, the ego is at the same time separated and cut off
from itself. It can never, as ego, contact, know or have itself in
full and genuine in-dividuality. Every such attempt removes
it as an ever regressing subject from its own grasp, leaving
simply some object semblance of itself. Continually elusive to
itself, the ego has itself merely as object. Divided and dissociated in its centeredness, it is beyond its own reach, obstructed, removed and alienated from itself. Just in having
itself, it does not have itself.

As with its awareness of itself, so with its awareness and having of its world—which is, actually, one dimension of its awareness of itself—the very having is a not-having. In the ego's awareness and having of its world, the world is always object. Reflectively, in its subjectivity, the ego may conceive of the world as the totality in which it itself is included. As, however, the reflected aspect of itself included in that world is an object aspect, so, too, is the world so conceived object to the ego as subject-conceiver. Whether in direct awareness or in conceptualization, the world is object, from which the ego as subject is left distant, apart, and estranged.

It is precisely this—the dichotomy of its subject-object structure—which constitutes the inherent existential ambiguity, conflict, and, indeed, contradiction of the ego in ego-consciousness. Bifurcated and disjoined in its unity, it is delimited by, but can not be sustained or fulfilled in, itself. Isolated and excluded in its relatedness, it is restricted to, yet shut off from, a world in which and to which it belongs. Having and not having, at once bound to and conditioned by, and at the same time separated and cut off from, itself and its world, the ego is rent by a double cleavage, split within as well as without. Never pure subject in its subjectivity, never absolutely free in its freedom, it is neither the ground nor the source of itself or its world, both of which it has, but neither of which it ever completely has. This is the predicament of the ego in ego-consciousness. This is the misery of man in human existence.

The existential expression of this predicament is the ego's double anxiety about having to live and having to die. The anxiety of having to live and the anxiety of having to die are but two expressions of the one fundamental root-anxiety: the anxiety with regard to overcoming the gnawing inner cleavage and contradiction which prevents the ego from fully being itself. The anxiety relating to life stems from the necessity to contend with and resolve this contradiction. The anxiety relating to death arises from the possibility that life may end before a resolution has been attained. Only the ego in ego-consciousness confronts, in order "to be," the need to find and fulfill itself. This is an inherent imperative which is not yet present to the infant, never quite present to the idiot, hardly more than semi-present to the "wolf-child," and perhaps no longer entirely present to the psychotic. As regards the natural completeness of the animal, however, it is wholly non-existent.

It would be meaningless—assuming it possible, and articulate language not to be itself an outgrowth of ego-consciousness—to ask a young animal, for example, a kitten, what it intends or would like to be when it grows up. But the human child encounters within as well as without exactly this question. For simple biological or physiological growth or maturation does not as such constitute the growth, maturation, or fulfillment of the human as human. Undoubtedly, motherhood comprises more of a measure of fulfillment for the human female than does fatherhood for the human male. Consequently, the answer of the little girl, "I am going to be a mother," is accepted as appropriate. Whereas, if the little boy were to reply, "I am going to be a father," this would not be considered responsive and could arouse some consternation.

Still, acknowledging immediately that its connotation extends far beyond the merely biological, human motherhood does not encompass final realization of the human female as human. In fact, no role, function, or vocation can ever ultimately satisfy the human—male or female—as human. The ego, however, constrained by its inner contradiction to seek its completion, is beguiled by that contradiction into just this deception.

Available to itself—even as it contemplates its own subjectivity—only in terms of some object cast of itself, the ego naturally comes to confuse being fulfilled with "being something." In its attempt as subject to cope with its task of finding itself, it envisages some object-image of itself. Through this image it hopes at once to be able both to prove itself and to gain recognition and approval from the other, or, if not the allegiance of, then to gain control over or at least independence of the other. For in its double alienation the ego encounters the absolute limitation imposed upon it by the subjectivity of the other as a challenge or, indeed, a threat.

Relying on its projected object-image to establish itself and overcome this threat, the ego may be led to take that limited, finite impression alone to be the whole of itself, its ground, its source, and its ultimate meaning, by which it is to be sustained, and through which it is to be fulfilled. Most or perhaps all of its subjectivity is now devoted and, in effect, subordinated to the content, or contents, necessary to realize the vision—wealth, power, prestige, masculinity, femininity, knowledge, moral perfection, artistic creativity, physical beauty, popularity, individuality, or "success." Virtually identifying with these contents, it focuses exclusively upon them and upon the conception of itself which they constitute. In this fixation and attachment it easily falls prey to the arch delusion of egocentricity. Ever in search of, yet ever elusive to, itself, the ego, object-dependent and object-obstructed, comes to be object-dominated and object-deluded.

Whether the object-image envisioned becomes actual or remains fanciful and idealized, the basic deception involved is the same. The ego in its totality is never merely any object-feature of itself or its actualized subjectivity—its body, mind, talents, position, "personality," goodness, profession or vocation, social or biological function, class, culture, nation, or race. However truly great the husband, wife, parent, ruler, scientist, thinker, artist, professional or business man—or woman, however much richer such an ego is, however much more it has itself, it does not have itself fully as ego, nor has it realized itself ultimately as human.

Expressing genuine subjectivity in going out of and giving itself in love, creativity, devotion to an ideal, or dedication to a task, it continues to be bound to and dependent upon the particular object element of that expression—the specific loved one, artistic activity, ideal, profession, or work. Perpetually enthralled in the inherent predicament of conditioned subjectivity, incapable of being a subject without an object, it is immediately circumscribed and curtailed by the object. Hence the ambivalence—in *erōs* or *philia*—of the hidden or open hostility toward that which is loved. This hostility, as well as the pride and special interest of the ego as subject in the love (or creativity, or morality), corrupts and defiles that love (creativity, and morality), provoking within the ego deep-rooted qualms of its own impurity, guilt, or, if religiously oriented, sin.

The ego, requiring an object to be a subject, can never attain complete fulfillment in or through any object. Such fulfillment, while authentic, is still limited, temporary, and tarnished. Despite the true richness of its creative subjectivity, the actual abundance of the contents of its life, the real greatness of its accomplishments and successes, the ego as ego is left unfulfilled. Unable to sustain itself within itself, and perhaps tormented by feelings of its own undeservedness, guilt, or sin, it comes to know melancholy and despondent moments of loneliness, frustration, or despair. Inwardly plagued by restlessness, insecurity, or a contempt and even hatred of itself, outwardly it possibly manifests any number of psychological or psychosomatic disturbances.

Yet often the ego manages to contain these pangs of disquietude and to finish out its life in just this condition. But even as it does so, it is under the continual threat that the smoldering deep-seated uneasiness may erupt and surge forth in an anguish and dread which is uncontainable. This could occur should the ego no longer be able to rationalize away its sense of unworthiness or its sense of guilt, should it become morbidly uncertain of the divine forgiveness of its sin, or should the components necessary to maintain its object-image otherwise come to be lost, destroyed, or unavailable, or, while remaining, prove disillusioning, grow empty, or simply cease to be engaging. Finally, some ordinary occurrence in daily life can bring the abrupt traumatic realization that not only is every possible content transitory and ephemeral, but so, too, is the ego itself. Ever vulnerable, in youth as well as in age, to illness and infirmity in body and mind, it must die.

Intellectually, the inevitability of its death is, of course, known to the ego all along. Actually experiencing, however, the prospect of its own non-being as a shattering existential shock in effect utterly destroys the illusion as to the possibility of its consummation in terms of any object-image. The traumatic anxiety about having to die is acutely poignant testimony to the final inability of any object aspect or object content to satisfy the human ultimately as human. Caught fully and apprehensively in the double anxiety of having to live and having to die, the ego undergoes the excruciating torment of the most piercing indecision of all: to be or not to be.

This singularly probing misgiving—the uncertainty of the ego whether to endure any longer its struggle for fulfillment— is, perhaps, the profoundest expression of its plight: nothing it can do can resolve its contradiction. As long as the ego remains simply as ego, the contradiction inherent in it also remains.

In open and honest recognition of its strait, the ego may have the courage and strength to take its negativities upon itself and continue to strive "to be." Although frequently an effort of heroic character, this still does not constitute positive realization. An affirmative expression of meaningful subjectivity in accepting, bearing, and suffering, the fulfillment adumbrated is, at best, latent and anticipatory rather than actual. At worst it again becomes delusive, involving, in this instance, a subject-delusion.

In enduring and withstanding, the ego sometimes thinks it to be itself assuming and sustaining total responsibility for itself and its existence. Forgetting that as object it is a passive, given fact beyond appropriation by its own acts or decisions as subject, it succumbs to the delusion of *hybris*. Blinded by this delusion, it dares, even in the throes of the overwhelming catastrophes of its life, to declare, nonetheless, that it is "the master of its fate," that it is "the captain of its soul."

This deception, moreover, is usually maintained only through the suppression of any emotion, warmth, compassion, or love. The same ego-will which disciplines and steels itself against its negativities often comes to be rigid, brittle, and unyielding, fearful of ever relaxing its tautness lest it collapse completely. Yet, it is exactly this unremitting strain which keeps it continually precarious, under the constant threat of snapping and breaking down. Overwrought, over-responsible, and over-repressed, it may abruptly abandon itself to just the opposite extreme.

In contrast to taking upon itself and forbearing the negativity of its predicament, the ego instead undertakes to avoid or disavow that negativity. It attempts "to be" not in spite of, but in disregard of, its limitations as a conditioned subject. Held in the bondage of an object-dependence and object-constriction, the ego endeavors to escape—rather than bear—that bondage by refusing to acknowledge the seriousness of, by contriving to forget, or by presuming to deny altogether the object aspect as such.

Ignoring the nature or components of its acts and decisions, the ego would now immerse itself in a flood of doing, acting, and deciding—either in search of distraction, or else exclusively for the sake of doing, acting, and deciding. In the latter case, seeking to realize a pure subjectivity free from all object constraints, the ego, misled by an implied fallacy of reductionism, falls into a double delusion. While assuming that as active subject its sheer subjectivity will reduce the object aspect, it fears that unless it is continuously active as subject, it will itself be reduced to object.

Whatever the motivation, however, subjectivity denuded of the seriousness of its object content ceases to be meaningful subjectivity. It quickly degenerates into aimless doing simply to "keep busy," vacuous "having fun," impulsive spontaneity, indulgent assertiveness, irresponsible non-conformity, wanton caprice, or unbridled libertinism and licentiousness. In any instance, such subjectivity is unable to provide other than diversionary interests and satisfactions or momentary and fleeting "thrills," and even these gratifications steadily weaken and begin to turn acrid and arid in the next moment. In frenzied desperation, the ego is driven to heighten the intensity of this supposed subjectivity—more and more doing, more and more pleasure-seeking, more and more non-conformity, more and more "getting away from it all," more and more narcotics, alcohol, and sex and its perversions.

The process is pathetically vicious. Incapable of being eradicated, the object aspect inherent in the subject-object structure of the ego is only rendered further and further poverty-stricken, destitute, and useless, while the subjectivity of the ego, denied in turn any significant object element, becomes increasingly meaningless, empty, and dissolute. Unmindful of the fact that it can never be a subject unless it also is or has an object, the ego, in its attempt to reduce the object aspect through an irresponsible abandonment to subjectivity, succeeds merely in reducing itself as a whole. Left ensnared in the very impasse it had sought to avert, it still has looming before it the abyss and despair of the yawning inner hiatus which frustrates and thwarts it from fully being itself.

Having failed in its alternate endeavors "to be," unable to tolerate the anxiety or the burden of a continued contending with this seemingly impossible task, the ego may have the temptation—even the compulsion—to give up all further effort. Virtually choosing "not to be," in the power of its subjectivity, it undertakes to elude its strait by abandoning that subjectivity. Whether through religious or secular idolatry, cynical negative indifference, slavish submission to collective conformity, psychological regression to the unawakened dependency of its infancy, or outright psychotic disintegration, the ego would evade its predicament by surrendering its freedom and responsibility, and with them itself as an authentic subject.

For the human as human, that is, for the ego in ego-consciousness, this, too, entails a dual deception. While forsaking subjectivity is still an expression of subjectivity, the ego in ceasing to be a true subject ceases to be a true ego. Any relinquishment by the ego of its subjectivity necessarily involves the diminution, impairment, or loss of itself as ego. In the blind superstition or obsequiousness of idolatry, in the nihilistic denial of the meaning and value of whatever act or decision, in the abject adjustment to the crowd, in the attempted return to the womb, or in the retreat and withdrawal into a psychosis, the human as human is negated or even destroyed. Abandonment of subjectivity is as delusive as abandonment to subjectivity.

Finally, no longer able to cope with, endure, or escape its plight, the ego, out of an agonizing sense of helplessness in its felt *aporia,* may choose "not to be" not through abandonment of its subjectivity, but through abandonment of itself. In the overwhelming anguish and despondency of the unviability and apparent unresolvability of its basic contradiction—in whichever of its manifestations—the ego directly undertakes its own annihilation in suicide.

Thus, whether exploring efforts toward resolution, acceptance, avoidance, or abandonment, the attempts by the ego to deal with its intrinsic contradiction are, at best, under the constant threat of collapse, transitory, partial, or fragmentary, and, at worst, under a deception or delusion, nihilistic and destructive. Not that any single mode is ever pursued exclusively. In its actual life the ego usually combines several, in varying degrees, and with varying predominances. All, however, positive or negative, responsible or irresponsible, profound or superficial, stem ultimately from the one fundamental longing of the ego, caught in the inner and outer alienation and estrangement of its inherent contradiction, to find and to fulfill, to really know, to come home to and to fully be and have itself in and with its world. This longing and its quest for fulfillment constitute the central and ultimate concern of the ego in ego-consciousness. This quest and this fulfillment constitute the existential beginning and the final end of Zen Buddhism.

According to its tradition, Zen, or Ch'an,[2] Buddhism in effect began in China when a perplexed sixth-century Chinese, Shen-kuang, discontent with his learned and erudite Confucian and Taoist study, heard of the presence at a nearby Buddhist temple of a Zen teacher from India and undertook to visit him. The Indian master, Bodhidharma, sitting crossed-legged facing a wall, continued sitting and did not receive the caller. Shen-kuang, resolute out of a deep disquietude, kept returning. Finally, one night he remained standing there throughout a heavy snow storm, until, at dawn, the snow reached his knees. Moved, Bodhidharma inquired the purpose of this action. In tears, the Chinese begged the Indian teacher, would he not grant the benefit of his wisdom to help troubled beings. Bodhidharma replied that the way was unbearably difficult, involving the greatest trials, and not to be attained by those lacking in perseverance or determination. Hearing this, Shen-kuang took out a sword he was carrying, cut off his left arm, and placed it in front of the Indian monk. Only in that moment did Bodhidharma accept him as a student, giving him the new name Hui-k'o.[3]

Venturing to interpret this account—very likely legendary—in what may be considered its symbolic significance for an understanding of Zen Buddhism, one first notes that an unsettled and distraught ego moves toward the teacher. The Zen master waits, as it were, for a questing ego to come to him. Even then he is apt not to accord direct recognition. On the surface, his initial response sometimes appears to be slighting or discouraging. This seeming inattentiveness, or even rejec-

---

2 *Ch'an* is the first syllable of the Chinese *ch'an-na*, (pronounced in Japanese *zenna*) a transliteration of the Sanskrit, *dhyāna*, a kind of "concentration" or "contemplation."

3 This rendition is taken from the *Ching-te Ch'uan-teng Lu* (The Record of the Transmission of the Lamp), vol. 3.

tion, is, however, but a mode of probing the seriousness of the quest. When the master has been convinced of the ultimacy of that seriousness, open acknowledgment and reception are immediately forthcoming.

It is, indeed, just the all-compelling and unrelenting existential plight leading him to approach and to keep returning to Bodhidharma, to expose himself to a snow storm, and to cut off his own arm which establishes Hui-k'o symbolically as the first Zen "student." Perturbed and distressed in his inner contradiction, unrelieved by classical learning, Hui-k'o goes to Bodhidharma in search of alleviation and resolution, and is ready, in that pursuit, to stake his total being.

Whatever the historicity of this incident, it is precisely this root-fundamental quest born of the inherent human predicament which constitutes, when brought before a Zen teacher, the existential beginning of Zen Buddhism. Without it, although one sit in crossed-legged meditation for decades at innumerable Zen temples, engaging in countless interviews with a myriad of Zen masters, one remains, notwithstanding, a student of Zen in name alone. For Zen Buddhism, finally, neither is in itself nor does it offer any objective, substantive content to be studied as such psychologically, religiously, philosophically, historically, sociologically, or culturally. The only valid component of Zen Buddhism is one's own concrete life and existence, its basic contradiction and incompleteness, and, in distinction to the mere longing, the actual quest for reconciliation and fulfillment. If what goes under the designation of Zen Buddhism does not, in fact, deal with and undertake to resolve the intrinsic existential plight of the ego in ego-consciousness, despite any claims it may make to "orthodoxy," it is no longer authentic Zen Buddhism.

Accepted as a genuine Zen student, Hui-k'o then inquired after the truth. Bodhidharma declared it was not to be found outside of oneself. Hui-k'o, nevertheless, bared his plaint. His heart-mind was not at peace, and he implored the master to pacify it.

Here is further confirmation that Hui-k'o's impelling vexation stemmed from his inner contradiction. The Chinese term, *hsin,* rendered as heart-mind, can mean heart or mind, but is more than either alone. The Greek, *psyche,* or the German, *Geist,* probably approach it more closely. In the terminology of this presentation, it may be taken to be the ego as subject. The ego as subject, in its situation of conditioned subjectivity, plagued by disquietude and unrest, pleads for pacification.

Bodhidharma, in anticipation, had already begun his guidance and instruction in declaring that a resolution could not be gained from the outside. Not yet comprehending, and, perhaps, out of felt helplessness, or even desperation, Hui-k'o persisted and presented his plight, requesting Bodhidharma to alleviate it.

What was Bodhidharma's response? Did he delve into Hui-k'o's past—his personal history, parents, early childhood, when he first began to sense the disturbance, the cause, symptoms, and attending circumstances? Did he explore Hui-k'o's present—his occupation, marital status, dreams, likes, and interests? Bodhidharma's reply was: "Bring forth your heart-mind and I shall pacify it for you!" [4]

Eschewing all the particularities of Hui-k'o's life, past or present, Bodhidharma plunged immediately and directly into the living core of the human predicament itself. The ego, caught in the clutches of its own intrinsic contradiction and split, which it can neither resolve nor endure, is challenged to produce not anything it may feel to be its problem, but itself as apparent sufferer of the problem. Bring forth the ego-subject which is troubled! Bodhidharma, and Zen Buddhism after him, realizes that, finally and fundamentally, it is not that the ego has a problem, but that the ego is the problem. Show me who it is who is disturbed and you shall be pacified.

Beginning thus with Bodhidharma and continuing ever thereafter, the basic, unveering approach of Zen Buddhism, whatever the special form or mode of its methodology in word, deed, or gesture, has been just such a straightforward, concrete assault upon the contradictory dualistic subject-object structure of the ego in ego-consciousness. The sole and exclusive aim has remained throughout to overcome the divisive inner and outer cleavage separating and removing the ego from itself— and its world—in order that it may fully be and truly know who and what it is.

[4] *Ching-te Ch'uan-teng Lu,* vol. 3.

Hui-neng (7th century), after Bodhidharma the second great figure in the annals of Zen, being visited by a monk, asked simply but pointedly, "What is it which thus comes?" [5] It is recorded that it took the monk, Nan-yo, eight years before he could answer.[6] On another occasion, this same Hui-neng inquired: "What is your original face prior to the birth of father and mother?" [7] That is, what are you beyond the subject-object structure of your ego in ego-consciousness?

Lin-chi (9th century), founder of one of the two major schools of Zen Buddhism still extant in Japan,[8] where he is known as Rinzai, once charged:

"There is one true man without a title on the mass of red-coloured flesh; he comes out and goes in through your sense gates. If you have not yet borne witness to him, look, look!"

A monk came forward and asked, "Who is this true man without a title?"

Rinzai came down from his chair and taking hold of his chest demanded, "Speak, speak!"

The monk hesitated, whereupon, letting him go, Rinzai exclaimed, "What kind of dirt-scraper is this true man without a title!" So saying, Rinzai went back to his room, leaving the monk to chew the cud." [9]

To help the ego awaken to and realize this "true man without a title," that is, to fully be and truly know itself, there arose among certain Zen teachers—notably those of the Lin-chi or Rinzai School—the use of what is known, in Japanese, as the koan.[10] This is a development especially of the eleventh and twelfth centuries, when Zen, or Ch'an, Buddhism, having acquired great esteem and wide renown throughout China, attracted many who no longer came out of any compelling existential need. Earlier masters would probably have reacted with the same outward indifference and disregard as did Bodhidharma. These later teachers, however, in the sincere and compassionate desire to help all inquirers, began, now,

---

[5] *Wu-teng Hui-yüan* (A Composite of the Five Lamps), vol. 3.
[6] *Ibid.*
[7] *Shūmon Kattō Shū* (A Collection of "Zen Complications").
[8] The other is the *Ts'ao-tung* (in Japanese, *Sōtō*) School.
[9] Quoted from Daisetz T. Suzuki, *Living By Zen* (Tokyo, Sanseido, 1949), p. 23.
[10] In Chinese, *kung-an*, literally, public document or testament.

themselves to initiate their relation to the caller by means of a koan.

The Chinese Sung master first to employ the koan somewhat systematically, Ta-hui (12th century), on one occasion spoke as follows:

Whence are we born? Whither do we go? He who knows this whence and whither is the one to be truly called a Buddhist. But who is this one who goes through this birth-and-death? Again, who is the one who knows not anything of the whence and whither of life? Who is the one who suddenly becomes aware of the whence and whither of life? Who is the one, again, who, facing this koan, cannot keep his eyes fixed, and as he is not able to comprehend it, feels his internals altogether put out of order as if a fiery ball swallowed down could not readily be ejected. If you wish to know who this one is, apprehend him where he cannot be brought within the fold of reason. When you thus apprehend him, you will know that he is after all above the interference of birth-and-death.[11]

The ultimate objective remains the same: to know and apprehend who one is beyond "the fold of reason," that is, beyond the subject-object structure of intellection. Toward this end the koan, a kind of question, problem, challenge, or demand presented by and upon the initiative of the master, is intended to serve a twofold function. The first is to penetrate to the depths and quicken at its source the deeply buried or deceptively concealed basic underlying concern of the ego in ego-consciousness. The second is, while stirring this fundamental longing and its quest, to keep them properly rooted and directed. For it is not sufficient that they simply be aroused. They must, in order to avoid the many deceptive and delusive pitfalls in which they may become attenuated or go astray, also be carefully guided and even fostered.

In the earlier or pre-koan phase of Zen Buddhism, the caller generally came out of the provocation of his own life experience, already bestirred by some existentially oppressing perplexity. Normally, however, the "question" or concern had not yet been plumbed to its ultimate depth. Although kindled naturally, known neither in its root-source nor in its true nature, and hence without an adequate form, it could easily be-

11 Quoted from Suzuki, *Living By Zen*, pp. 171-72.

come veiled or deflected. Despite a genuine intensity and seriousness, the longing and quest were thus usually blind, amorphous, and confused, requiring a correct grounding and focus.

When, in this period, the student, during an encounter with the master, would receive a piercing challenge or demand—for instance, "Bring forth your heart-mind!" "What is it which thus comes?" "What is your original face prior to the birth of father and mother?" "When you are dead, cremated, and the ashes scattered, where are you?" [12] or, simply, "Speak! Speak!"—the effect, often, was to provide just the needed orientation and guidance. Even so, such challenges, questions, or demands were not called koans. These spontaneous, unstructured exchanges between master and student were instead termed *mondō*, or, in Chinese, *wen-ta,* literally, question and answer. But since these *mondō*-exchanges did prompt, ground, and direct the radical and ultimate concern of the ego, many of them were actually used, subsequently, either as koans, or as the basis of koans.

The koan in its double function may therefore be considered a deliberate and calculated attempt to secure a result previously obtained naturally and without contrivance. Conversely, it can perhaps be said, regardless of the technical terminology and distinctions of Zen Buddhism itself, that the earlier student had his own natural koan, natural as to the burning substance, although still to be given a proper form or focus, whereas, in the later period, when the inquirer approached neither with a suitable form of the question nor yet existentially fired to its all-consuming content, the master himself sought to foster both by initially presenting such a "question," as it were, from the outside. In this instance, the koan, rather than being partially natural, was totally given.

But again, it must be emphasized immediately that as long as the "question" or koan continues to be "on the outside" or "given," the effort is futile, and there is, finally, no Zen Buddhism. In its character and structure, however, as well as in the mode of its application and usage, the koan is carefully designed as a safeguard against precisely this danger. For by its very nature the koan does not permit itself to be fitted into any dualistic subject-object scheme of the ego in ego-consciousness.

[12] Quoted from Suzuki, *Living By Zen*, p. 189, n. 5.

It can never even be meaningful, much less be "solved" or satisfied, and remain an object external to the ego as subject. This is strikingly illustrated by one of the most widely given "first" koans, *"Mu,"* or, in Chinese, *"Wu."*

The basis of this koan, like that of so many others, is a previously recorded *mondō*-exchange. The ninth-century Chinese master, Chao-chou (Japanese, Jōshū), once being asked if a dog had Buddha-nature, replied "Mu!" (taken in its literal sense, "It has not!"). As a formal, given koan, however, this one syllable response is completely removed from the narrow confines of the initial inquiry, and presented—simply by itself—for the student to "see," or to "become." The koan is, "See *mu!*" or "Become *mu!*" Clearly, this can have no significance and can in no way be handled, dealt with, or realized within the framework of any subject-object dualism.

Similarly, when the koan is taken from one of the aforementioned *mondō*-exchanges, "What is your original face prior to the birth of father and mother?" or when it is the koan later preferred to *"Mu"* by the eighteenth-century Japanese master, Hakuin, because it contained more of a noetic element, "Hear the sound of one hand!", these problems or challenges can never be answered or met, and, indeed, have no meaning within the subject-object structure of ego-consciousness, its intellection, or logic. Whatever the noetic element which the koan may, in effect, have, to come to its "resolution" or "understanding" is impossible if it is aproached as an object-question or object-problem by the ego as subject, epistemological or otherwise.

Whether *"Mu,"* the "sound of one hand," "Where are you after you have been cremated?" or one's "original face," the koan, natural or given, offers nothing tangible, nothing to grasp, nothing to take hold of as object. Should the student try to objectify it, under the careful and alert master his maneuver is sharply repudiated and the supposed "solution" uncompromisingly rejected.

Sometimes, however—for example in the "koan system" as it has developed in Japan—some object aspect of the form or content of the particular koan may yet remain in the accepted presentation. To filter this out and to broaden and deepen the still limited realization, the student is given another koan.

and then another, and another. Improperly applied, this "koan system" becomes its own impediment and eventually succumbs to the very danger which the koan originally was intended to guard against.

The only valid content of the koan is the contending ego itself. The genuine quest to "solve" the koan is the quest of the split and divided ego to come to its own reconciliation and fulfillment. Considered from the side of its origination, the koan is, itself, an expression of that fulfillment. Whether he initially realizes it or not, the authentic struggle with the koan is the struggle of the student to fulfill himself. In either case—natural or given—this koan effort must continue delusive or vain if undertaken by the ego as subject venturing to deal with or handle its problem as object. For, as has already been seen, it is exactly the existential dichotomy between subject and object which is the problem of the ego.

Zen Buddhism, however, usually has not tried to explain this intellectually, conceptually, or analytically, as I have attempted to do. Zen rather prefers to hit the ego solidly and directly—in the natural *mondō*-exchange or in the formal, given koan—with challenges and demands which the ego in its subject-object disjunction can never meet. These assaults, through expressions of consummate fulfillment in word, deed, or gesture, constitute Zen's own peculiar and unique mode of concretely declaring—and endeavoring to get the ego to grasp—that in no way can the ego ever complete itself within itself, that it can not possibly—in terms of its subject-object structure—resolve the contradiction which is this very subject-object structure itself.

The preliminary objective of the koan is, therefore, to impel and incite not merely noetically, but affectively and physically as well, what in the terminology of Zen Buddhism is called the "great doubt" [13]—and to do so in such a way that the ego becomes totally and existentially the "great doubt block" [14] itself. Unless the ego does come to be the "great doubt block" itself, it can not be said to have arrived at the "great doubt."

Toward this provisional end, as well as toward its final end, the koan was combined with the already existing practice—in

[13] *Ta-i;* in Japanese *daigi* or *taigi.*
[14] *Ta-i-t'uan;* in Japanese, *daigidan* or *taigidan.*

Zen methodology—of sitting crossed-legged in a form of sustained "concentration," called, in Japanese, *zazen*.[15] This discipline of seating oneself with legs crossed, each foot upon the opposite thigh, spinal column straight, and hands folded or overlapping in front, in a kind of "contemplation" or "meditation" was prevalent in India long before Buddhism. It was supposedly in this posture that Śākyamuni came to his own fulfillment. It was also in this position that Bodhidharma was reported to have been seated when visited by Hui-k'o. But a century later Hui-neng rebelled against what he recognized to be the purely formalistic and quietistic corruption of this practice. Accordingly, not too much mention of it is made immediately following him. Nonetheless, it is generally agreed that Zen monks and students of the period must all have taken to it at some time or another.

With the natural koan, the inner dynamic of this "concentration" derives from one's own internal disturbance and disquietude. The focus and direction is most apt to be that provided by the master during a recent interview or exchange. The student, after such an encounter, is very likely to carry its effect into the "meditation hall"[16] and sit with it in *zazen*.

In the case of the formal, given koan, however, the ego, not yet roused to the same compelling intensity of its plight, often still lacks the necessary "concentrating" power to "attack" the koan. Thus there arose alongside of the koan and *zazen*, in the Lin-chi or Rinzai school, especially in Japan, what are known, in Japanese, as the *sesshin*[17] and *sanzen*.[18]

Depending on the monastery, one week of the month six or eight times a year is devoted entirely by the monk or student to *zazen*—and his koan. Arising usually at 3 A.M., he continues in this *zazen*—except for light work chores, sutra-chanting, meals, a lecture, interviews with the master, and short rest periods, which may be omitted—until 10 P.M., or later, for seven consecutive days. This period is called a *sesshin*, and the

---

15 In Chinese, *tso-ch'an*, literally, "sitting-*dhyāna*," but perhaps better rendered as "Zen sitting."

16 *Ch'an-t'ang*; in Japanese, *zendō*, literally, "Zen-hall."

17 In Chinese, *she* (sometimes, *chieh*)-*hsin* "concentralization of the heart-mind" or "heart-mind concentralization."

18 In Chinese, *ts'an-ch'an*, "to pursue the Zen-quest."

daily compulsory and voluntary visits—from two to five—to the master, *sanzen*.[19]

Under the stimulation of such a regimen with its taut and serious atmosphere, the given koan may begin to take effect. The student, prodded by the stick of the head monk when dozing comes upon him, exertion wanes, or stiffness and tiredness set in, and spurred, inspired, goaded or even driven by the master, finds himself to be more and more caught by his koan. As his each response to it presented is rejected, he becomes increasingly dislodged, shaken, and unsteady in whatever assurance or complacency he originally had. Gradually, having less and less to offer, yet persistently pressed with the same unrelenting demand for an "answer," the student grappling with the koan, unable as a some-one to deal with his problem as a some-thing, encounters the exact frustration and despair known by the ego in its natural quest to fulfill itself.

The inability of the koan to be resolved as an object by the ego as subject is, in fact, precisely the inability of the ego as ego in its subject-object bifurcation to resolve the existential contradiction which is that bifurcation. For the student, the given koan, also, is now, like the natural koan, a mode or expression of the actual "question" or quandary of the ego itself, and the struggle for its "solution" an equally torturing life-and-death struggle. The koan thus comes to be, as regards the student, a living crisis, taking over as the central and exclusive concern of his entire being. His confronting it is, indeed, his confronting his own predicament in all of its immediate and burning urgency. Not able to cope with it, he truly "feels his internals altogether put out of order as if a fiery ball swallowed down could not readily be ejected."

This accounts for one reason why the monk or student, when he has not yet arrived at a "determination," frequently refuses to see the teacher, and why, for the compulsory *sanzen* visits, he has sometimes to be beaten, pulled, dragged, or, as once was actually witnessed, forcibly carried by four other monks out of the meditation hall and into the interview.

The master's insistence upon a response to the koan does not issue in any sense from an external, strange, or heter-

[19] This account is broadly generic and presents none of the finer, more technical distinctions.

onomous authority. Quite the contrary. A genuine teacher is
an embodiment of the ultimate fulfillment of the agonizing
ego itself. His demand for a resolution of the koan, natural or
given, is, in reality, the longing and questing critical mandate
of the ego for its own resolution. The refusal to see the master
arises from the incapacity of the ego to face itself in its acute
lack and insufficiency—tellingly mirrored, as it were, by its
consummate completion in the person of the teacher. Staying away affords at least a temporary respite from having to
meet in full and uncompromising honesty the imperative of
its own inner conflict for mitigation and relief. Having had,
during the many previous audiences, its efforts and attempts,
whether partial, fragmentary, delusive, or deceptive, pared
away and discarded, the ego fights to keep itself sheltered and
to avoid not only the embarrassment of disclosure in its already
partial nakedness but also the torment of a further or complete
exposure in total nakedness. For the threat to the ego of such
a total naked exposure in its bared root-contradiction could
appear to it to be a threat to its very existence, carrying with it
the terror of possible insanity or death.

Expressed in more Zen-like metaphor, the ego, denied and
deprived the function of every other aspect and part of itself,
is left clinging by its teeth to a branch overhanging a precipice.
Holding on to this last remnant of itself, it feels that it can still,
at least for the present, preserve itself, albeit in an almost
intolerable condition. In this critical circumstance, to be forced
to encounter itself genuinely and authentically in the person of the teacher and receive the compelling commands:
"Speak!" and "Speak quick!" can be for it, indeed, a trying
ordeal. And this all the more so when it realizes that should it
undertake, before the master, to stay put and not respond, it
may even be prevented the use of those teeth. Somehow it
senses that, ultimately, this is an absolute necessity which, in
fact, it must undergo, but which, at the moment, it is not able
to undergo.

Not that this denying or proscribing by the master is ever a
simple nihilistic negation. What is methodically and rigorously
stripped away is that which the ego as subject is able to hold on
to or deal with as object. This also involves those contents
which could, or do, afford a limited or qualified fulfillment.

For as long as the ego as subject continues to be or cling to an object, its inner contradiction and predicament as ego remain. The aim is, therefore, to remove all available object-constituents—including the body itself—toward the end of baring and exposing in its naked contradiction the very subject-object structure of the ego as such. Without an object, the ego, unable to be a subject, becomes itself untenable. Yet, it is just to this radical and fundamental moment that Zen wishes to drive, and there to challenge, in the words of a contemporary teacher: "Without using your mouth, without using your mind, without using your body, express yourself!"

Pressed to this extremity, the nature of the student's quest and struggle begins to be altered. His *zazen*, hitherto undoubtedly a struggling with and a concentrating upon the natural or given koan as an object, is now, shorn of the objectified koan as well as of all other content, itself rendered objectless. This is but the culmination of the process started when the koan began to have its effect and to enter into the student's internals, eventually to permeate his whole being. Becoming less and less external, it became less and less accessible for ordinary contemplation or meditation. At last, it has been completely divested of every conceivable object aspect. Nevertheless, it still persists, unsettled and unresolved, and with it, the unremitting exhortation from the master, as from the ego itself, for settlement and resolution.

As with its koan, so with itself. The ego, in an existential quandary which it can neither compose, endure, abandon, or escape, is unable to advance, unable to retreat, unable to stand fixed. Nonetheless, it remains under the impelling admonition to move and to resolve. Thoroughly and systematically denuded, deprived of the use of all its powers, contents, resources, abilities, and, finally, its very body, it faces—notwithstanding—the commanding imperative of the teacher to present and express itself. In this apparent cul de sac the ego undergoes a felt anguish of utter futility and helplessness which ordinarily could lead to suicide. In the Zen situation, however, this anxiety and despair never become submerged into any such total negative hopelessness.

Unlike the ego in a pre-suicidal state, the student with a true master has before him the living assurance of a possible solution to his problem. The teacher, expressing the genuine love and compassion of ultimate reconciliation, not only bolsters and supports through that love, but existentially encourages and reassures simply by his being. The student somehow senses that the master is the student even more than the student is himself. In this he also feels the teacher to be bearing as much as himself the actual trial with its suffering and distress. The master is thus, for the student, the authority, affirmation, and love of the complete fulfillment of the student's very own existence.

The student, on the other hand, is for the teacher at once the teacher himself, although another, whom the teacher must, out of his love and compassion, thrust into the tormenting pit of the utterly raw and exposed inner contradiction. On his part, the master is obliged to tear away and probe into the central core of the wound, for only when fully laid bare and existentially realized can it heal.

As yet, the pain and anxiety of the ego in its ostensible prostration do not issue from the wound or contradiction directly, but derive from the ego as bearer of the wound. Denied, from without, all object content, the ego, from within, still not subjectless, and hence still not genuinely objectless, continues to hold on. Once, however, it can become the unwrought root-contradiction, then the contradiction supports and bears itself, and the exterior or simply felt negativity of the ego is left behind.

The preliminary objective, consequently, is for the ego, bodily as well as mentally, to come to be this radical contradiction or "great doubt block." The "great doubt" or "great doubt block" is no other than the intrinsic predicament of the ego in ego-consciousness totally and exhaustively exacerbated. The initial purpose of the koan—and the accompanying methodology of *zazen,* the *sesshin,* and *sanzen*—is to get the ego to arouse, to crystallize, to bring entirely to the fore, and then, rather than endure, to become wholly and authentically the living contradiction which, as ego, it veritably is.

In order that the ego thus be true to itself as ego, it must expend itself and actualize its ultimate limit not in terms of its external failures or impossibilities, but in terms of its inner structural antinomy. As an ever object-oriented subject, for the ego to approach this actualization it is usually necessary that every possible content for its object-orientation be spent, depleted, or denied. Unable as subject to make any further effort away from itself toward the outside, it may then undergo an internal transformation, not remaining as subject and simply reversing its orientation inwardly upon itself as object in introspection, but becoming, instead, radically and consummately, its inherent root-contradiction. Only when it has become fully that contradiction does it finally come to be subjectless and objectless. For as that core-contradiction, ego-consciousness is, itself, arrested and checked. Ceasing to be a fluid, conditioned subjectivity, it is now, without subjectivity or objectivity, one total, solid, existential block.

This is not, however, either the pre-ego-consciousness of the infant, the abortive ego-consciousness of the idiot, the retarded ego-consciousness of the "wolf-child," the deteriorated ego-consciousness of the psychotic, the numbed ego-consciousness of the anesthetized, the lethargic ego-consciousness of the stupor, the quiescent ego-consciousness of dreamless sleep, the suspended ego-consciousness of the trance, or the inert ego-consciousness of the coma. This is rather ego-consciousness itself, in and as its own radical contradiction, stayed and impacted. It is neither vacant nor blank, nor does it cancel itself and dissolve. While blocked and constricted, lacking active discrimination between subject and object, itself and not itself, it is not at all dull or lifeless. It is, indeed, most sensitive. Moreover, being as yet unresolved, its struggle continues, although no more by or of the ego merely as ego. Ego has at last become koan, and both have become the struggle and "concentration" itself, the "great doubt block" itself, the root-contradiction itself, subjectless and objectless.

This is the ego thoroughly exhausted as ego. No longer subject or object, it is unable to strive or attempt. In contradistinction to the only seeming helplessness of the pre-suicidal state, this is consummate existential helplessness itself, in which even suicide is impossible. As long as the ego as subject can undertake an act, albeit its own annihilation, it is not truly helpless.

Similarly, it is the ego acutely and genuinely its root-contradiction which constitutes the true dilemma, the true impasse, the true *cul de sac*, the true nihilism of valuelessness and meaninglessness, the true *aporia* of "no exit." This is the plight and the predicament of the ego utterly and conclusively excoriated, shorn of every veil and integument. This is ultimate negativity itself.

This ultimate negativity, while a necessary antecedent and not simply negative, is, however, still a precondition. It is not yet resolution or fulfillment. Becoming the "great doubt block," that is, the root-contradiction in its root, is not the final end.

No longer in its subject-object contradiction, the ego as that contradiction itself is wholly attenuated, disabled, and immobilized. Its being objectless and subjectless is a negativity of total bondage and obstruction, in which subject and object in their contradictory dualistic polarity completely impede and impound each other in one constricted, helpless clog. Being thus negatively subjectless and objectless, having neither mind nor body, is not sufficient. Without body, without mouth, and without mind, there must be expression. The root-contradiction or "great doubt block" remains to be radically and fundamentally broken up and resolved.

It is only, however, when this critical state of the "great doubt block" has been fully actualized that it can be uprooted. It is precisely in this condition of the most intense, most delicate tension, that some chance event of daily life, or, perhaps, some word, deed, or gesture of the master, can suddenly spark the basic and revolutionary upheaval in which this root-contradiction "great doubt block" instantaneously breaks up in what is at the same time a break-through.

Just as the ego in ego-consciousness is initially both an act and a fact, so its eruption and resolution also have the quality of act as well as of fact, but now neither relatively so nor merely of the ego as ego. For even as the root-contradiction "great doubt block," ordinary ego-consciousness is, in effect, already transcended. Although still a negative absence of distinction between subject and object, itself and not itself, as the "great doubt block," it encompasses the entire realm of being, including the very differentiation of being from non-being. As the root-contradiction in its root, it is the abyss of being, or, more properly, the abyss of the antinomy between being and non-being, existence and nonexistence. But, while negatively the contradiction and abyss, it is this same root-core which is—positively—the ground and the source.

Approached from the ego, this core is the ultimate extremity and final limit, the innermost center of the contradiction which is ego-consciousness. Actualized as this center, the ego is expended but not yet completely consumed. As long as it remains this root-core in terms of itself—even though exhausted—it continues to be that root negatively—as the root-limit, root-barrier, and root-impediment. As such, the ego is only "as if dead." When, however, this negative root-core, bursting, uproots and turns on itself, then the ego truly dies the "great death," [20] which is at once the great birth or "great awakening." [21]

The "great death" is the ego dying to itself in its radical negativity. In no sense a relative nihilistic destruction or expiration into a hollow void or nothingness, this abrupt uprooting and reversal is, rather, the break-up and dissipation of the contradiction, of the abyss, of the *aporia*. The annulment and negation of ultimate negativity, it is itself positive. The negative dissolution is at the same time a positive resolution. The ego negated as ego in the central contradiction of its ego-consciousness attains, through this negation, positively and affirmatively, its resolution and fulfillment. In dying to itself as ego, it is born and awakens to its Self as Self.

Again to be emphasized is that the root-contradiction in its root is not here any metaphysical or ontological postulate. It is a most urgent and burning actuality. So, its bursting and turning upon itself is also a concrete reality. Breaking up and dissolving as that root-core contradiction, the ego gains, with direct immediacy, reconciliation and completion. The constricted and obstructed ultimate limit is now the freely functioning primordial source and ultimate ground. No longer centered in the root-contradiction of initial ego-consciousness, it is, instead, centered in the ground and source of its Self. Root-limit, reversing and turning on itself, becomes root-source and root-ground. This radical, cataclysmic uprooting, turning, and reversing by, of, and at the root-core, is called, in Zen, in Japanese, *satori*.[22]

---

[20] *Ta-ssu;* in Japanese *taishi.*
[21] *Ta-wu;* in Japanese *daigo* or *taigo.*
[22] In Chinese *wu,* literally, awakening or apprehending.

The *satori* break-up and dissolution of the expended and arrested ego in its root-contradiction at the root is the awakening of the ego or the root to its ground and source in its Self. This awakening to its Self is at once the awakening of its Self. From the perspective of ego-consciousness in its core-contradiction "great doubt block," the total break-up, disintegration, and death is an awakening and break-through to its Self. But from the opposite perspective, the awakening and break-through to its Self is the awakening and opening up of its Self. This is, truly, Self-awakening: that which awakens is that which is awakened, that by which it is awakened, and that to which it is awakened. Act as well as fact, it is at the same time its Self the ground, root-source, and prius of act and fact.

As ground and source neither dynamic nor static, it is not, however, a dead identity or a vacuous, abstract universality or oneness. Nor is it a simple non-duality or a "false sameness." [23] Although its Self the ground, source, and prius of the static and dynamic, it never remains in its Self, but is forever giving rise to expression of its Self. Indeed, awakened to its Self, it realizes that the very subjectivity of the ego as subject even in its contradictory duality, finally derives and springs from its Self. Similarly, the ultimate font of the longing and quest of the ego to overcome its alienation and estrangement and to complete and fulfill itself is also precisely its Self. Broken off from its Self, it longs and quests to return to its Self. The ego in its dual contradiction of having yet not having itself and its world, is, in fact, in the plight of having yet not having its Self.

In initial ego-consciousness, in addition to being separated and removed as subject from itself, the other, and its world as object, the ego, further, is cut off and obstructed as ego from its own ground and source. Its individuality, fragmented from within and isolated from without, is ungrounded and, therefore, unsustainable. Such an individuality, rent within, dissociated without, and strange to its own source, can never genuinely know or affirm itself because it never is or has itself genuinely. Solely in dying to itself as ego and awakening to its Self as Self is its authentic, autonomous in-dividuality actualized for the first time. Ceasing to be mere ego, it is here

[23] *O-p'ing-teng;* in Japanese *akubyōdō.*

after what may be designated or characterized as Self-ego, or ego-Self.

The inherent predicament of the existentially contradictory dualistic subject-object structure of the ego in ego-consciousness is ultimately resolved only when that living root-contradiction breaks up and dies to itself at its root, awakening in resolution and fulfillment in and as its Self as Self-ego. Its Self as Self the ground of itself as ego, it is at last free from the split and cleavage of any inner or outer dualistic duality. No longer struggling "to be" out of the gulf and abyss of an unresolved, bifurcated core, it now both is and issues forth from its Self as the fount and wellspring of itself as subject and object.

Unlike the conditioned subjectivity of initial ego-consciousness, no more does object bind, obstruct, circumscribe, or curtail subject. Nor, as in the state of the "great doubt block," do subject and object immobilize each other in the depth of their contradictory duality. Uprooted and reversed in and at that contradictory core, they are henceforth rooted and centered in their ultimate source. Trans-rooted and trans-centered, they cease to impede in mutual contradiction and become, instead, the free flowing manifestation of that source.

From the perspective of the ground-source in and of its Self, precisely this free and continuous flow out of its Self as subject and object is its return, unhindered and unhampered, to its Self, through time, but in Eternity. Again, this is Self-manifestation: that which manifests is that which is manifested, that through which it is manifested, and that of which it is manifested.

From the perspective of the awakened subject, fully realized as the unfolding of its ultimate ground, it is pure or unconditioned Self-subject, as its object is pure or unconditioned Self-object. Just as subject is expression and function of its Self, so, too, is object equally expression and function of its Self. As pure, unconditioned subject and object, subject is, indeed, object, as object is, indeed, subject. Their duality, no longer contradictory or dualistic, is hereafter a reconciled non-contradictory, non-dualistic duality. Moving unobstructed and unimpeded in the absolute freedom of unconditioned subjectivity, subject mirrors object and is mirrored by object, as object mirrors subject and is mirrored by subject. That which mirrors is that which is mirrored, that from which it is mirrored, and that in which it is mirrored. Ego, ego-consciousness, and its subject-object duality, becoming trans-rooted, trans-centered and transformed, are now the non-contradictory, non-dualistic duality of ego-Self, or Self-ego.

As Self the source of itself as ego, Self-ego is at once with form as it is without form. It is formless [24] form. As inexhaustible ground, it is without any definite fixed form, which formlessness is also not a fixed form. Neither theoretical nor abstract, this formlessness is its Self the fountain-spring of form. Because formless, it is able, in actual existence, to give rise to, to express its Self in, and to be all forms.

In its awakened Self-awareness and fulfillment as Self-ego, it is and has the form of itself as Self-ego. As ground-source, however, it is never simply the form of itself as Self-ego. Itself and not-itself as form in space, ego-Self is its own being and its own non-being as existence in time. It is, indeed, realized *ecstasis,* beyond itself and not-itself, beyond its being and its non-being. It may assert in unconditional affirmation, "I am" and "I am not," "I am I" and "I am not I," "I am I because I am not I," "I am not I, therefore I am I." Unconditional Self-affirmation is, in fact, an unconditionally dynamic Self-affirmation-negation, or, Self-negation-affirmation. (This may be considered, as well, to be the nature—or *logos*—of Love.)

Further, reconciled to and completed in its Self as Self-ego, it is the other, as the other is its Self. Itself and other being but an aspect of the duality of subject and object, just as it is itself an unfolding of its Self, so, too, is the other equally an unfolding of its Self: "I am I," "Thou art thou," "I am thou," "Thou art I."

As with subject and object, itself and the other, so with itself and its world. "When I see the flower, I see my Self; the flower sees my Self; the flower sees flower; the flower sees its Self; my Self sees its Self; its Self sees its Self."

Here is living, creative Love in consummate activation and fulfillment, ever expressing its Self, ever that which is expressed. That which expresses is that which is expressed, that with which it is expressed, and that for which it is expressed. Here, alone, is total and unconditioned affirmation of subject and

---

[24] *Wu-hsiang;* in Japanese *musō.*

object, of itself, of the other, of the world, of being, for here, alone, is total and unconditioned affirmation of its Self, by its Self, through its Self as Self-ego.

Now it is and knows its "original face" prior to the birth of its parents. Now it sees *"Mu,"* hears "the sound of one hand," and can present its Self "without using its body, mouth, or mind." Now it apprehends who and where it is "after its cremated ashes have been scattered."

This, finally, is human existence completed and fulfilled beyond the existential contradiction of its initial ego-consciousness. This, at last, is Man ultimately realized as Man fully being and having him-Self and his world, able to "transform mountains, rivers, and the great earth, and reduce them into [him-] Self," and to "transform [him-] Self and turn it into mountains, rivers, and the great earth." [25]

This, in my limited understanding, is the relation of Zen Buddhism to the human situation.

[25] See Suzuki, *Living By Zen*, pp. 26-27.

INDEX

173